The young Spurgeon

Yours in Jesus

C. H. Spurgeon

The young Spurgeon

Peter Jeffery

 EVANGELICAL PRESS

EVANGELICAL PRESS,
12 Wooler Street, Darlington, Co. Durham, DL1 1RQ, England.

British Library Cataloguing in Publication Data available

ISBN 0 85234 293 4

Other books by Peter Jeffery:

All things new
Seeking God
Walk worthy
Firm foundations
Stand firm
Our present sufferings
Christian handbook
I will never become a Christian
Stepping stones ... a New Testament guide for beginners

Cover picture reproduced by courtesy of Spurgeon's College

Printed in Great Britain by Bath Press, Avon

To Lorna

Contents

	Page
Preface	9
1. Early lessons	11
2. God's hand	19
3. Conviction of sin	27
4. Conversion	35
5. Experiences after conversion	47
6. Baptism	51
7. Serving the Lord	59
8. Waterbeach	71
9. The Calvinist	81
10. New Park Street	89
11. The work goes on	103
Postscript	111

Preface

The life of Spurgeon ought to be compulsory reading for all Christians, but Christians will not read much today. Consequently they are easily put off by the size of the two excellent volumes *The Early Years* and the *Full Harvest*. This is sad, but it is a fact that has to be faced. This short introduction into the life of the young Spurgeon is written to whet the appetites of Christians and encourage them to tackle the two-volume autobiography.

Peter Jeffery

1.
Early lessons

'Young man,' said the preacher, addressing one member of his small congregation, 'you look very miserable, and you will always be miserable if you do not obey my text.' The fifteen-year-old boy could have been offended by such a personal application from the pulpit, but he was not. On many occasions he had heard better preachers and better sermons, but never had he heard God speaking to him as on that never to be forgotten morning in Colchester. It seemed that all his young life he had been searching for a real and deep experience of God. His background and upbringing could have led him to assume that he was a Christian, but his heart told him it was not so. The Bible, which he knew well, confirmed that he had to be born again. But how and when? The answer came in the most unexpected place, from the most unexpected human source, but unmistakably it was God saying to him, 'Look unto me and be ye saved.'

The young man was Charles Haddon Spurgeon and the date was 6 January 1850. That first Sunday of the new year he had intended to go with his father to worship in Tollesbury, but the weather was so cold and the snow so thick that the nine-mile journey was ruled out. To most teenagers who are not Christians, this could have been an ideal excuse not to go to church at all. The young Spurgeon was different. Even though he was only fifteen, for many years he had known a deep longing to

be saved. This was not something casual or a passing child-
hood fad, for often he would be up at sunrise in order to seek
the Lord. His young voice cried out to God, 'Lord save me: it
will glorify thy grace to save such a sinner as I am! Lord save
me, O Lord, for Jesus died; by his agony and bloody sweat, by
his cross and passion, save me!'

Such praying is more than the emotional cry of an im-
pressionable youngster. Here is evidence of the work of the
Holy Spirit in a soul. And whether it is the soul of a child or an
adult, the Spirit always creates a conviction of sin and a
desperate desire to be saved. God was at work in Charles long
before he was capable of being aware of it.

He was born in the Essex village of Kelvedon on 19 June
1834. Before his first birthday the family moved to Colchester
and four months later he was taken to live with his grandfather,
the Rev. James Spurgeon, in the village of Stambourne. The
old man lived there for fifty years and was the minister of the
Independent Church. Charles stayed with him until he was
nearly five years old.

It is not clear why his parents sent him to live with his
grandfather, but God's purpose in this is not difficult to see.
The influence of his grandfather's spiritual life and his doctrinal richness was to have a tremendous effect in moulding the
young Spurgeon into the mighty preacher that God was to use
so wonderfully in later years. Those first five years with his
grandfather, and the subsequent long summer holidays he
spent at Stambourne, taught Charles to think seriously and
deeply about God and the Scriptures.

A regular Sunday morning practice was for him to sit with
old James Spurgeon in the best parlour as he prepared for
preaching. The young child was given a copy of the *Evangelical Magazine* to keep him quiet but what really ensured quiet
for the preacher was the warning that if little Charles distracted
his grandfather, he might not be able to preach well, 'and then
— ah! what would happen, if poor people did not learn the way
to heaven?' His young mind fully understood that this was the
most important thing in the world. It was a truth that caused

The manse at Stambourne, where Spurgeon lived with his grandparents

him great anxiety until he was converted, and a truth that was to remain at the centre of his preaching throughout the rest of his life.

A thirst for knowledge

The preacher is a man who handles the Bible with reverence and care. He wants to know its meaning and is not satisfied with a mere casual reading. This again was a lesson Charles learnt in his very early days at Stambourne. When he was a very small boy he was allowed to read the Scriptures at family prayers. One day he read from Revelation about the bottomless pit. Immediately he wanted to know what this meant, but the old gentleman would give no satisfactory answer and told him to go on reading. He did so, but he was determined to have an answer. So every morning he chose the same passage to read, and every morning stopped and asked, 'What is the bottomless pit?' His plan was to weary his grandfather into giving him an answer. The process was successful, but the answer horrified him!

'There is a deep pit,' said old James Spurgeon, 'and the soul is falling down — oh, how fast it is falling! There! The last ray of light at the top has disappeared, and it falls on, on, on, and so it goes on falling, on, on, on, for a thousand years. Is it not near the bottom yet? Won't it stop? No, no, the cry is, "On, on, on". "I have been falling a million years; am I not near the bottom yet?" "No, you are no nearer the bottom yet; it is the bottomless pit." It is on, on, on, and so the soul goes on falling perpetually into a deeper depth still, falling for ever into "the bottomless pit", on, on, on, into the pit that has no bottom! Woe, without termination, without hope of its coming to a conclusion!'

This must have been a frightening description for a child to hear, but it burnt deep into his heart and mind the reality of biblical truths.

Spurgeon's grandfather, James Spurgeon

Books

In an old, rambling house like the manse at Stambourne there would be many fascinating hideaways for a young boy. Charles discovered in his grandfather's house what he called his 'gold-mine'. Upstairs, opening out of one of the bedrooms, was a small, dark room. It contained books, and to this young boy it was a treasure. Here he first met John Bunyan and his 'pilgrim'. The martyrs of church history and the teaching of the Puritans all came to him out of this special gold-mine. He wrote many years later, 'Out of the darkened room I fetched these old authors when I was still a youth, and never was I happier than when in their company. I wonder whether some other boy will love them, and live to revive that grand old teaching, which will yet be to England her salvation and blessing.' Here we see God fashioning the habits and the appetites of the preacher whom he will use to bring countless thousands to a saving experience of the Lord Jesus Christ.

In his later ministry there were several occasions when Spurgeon had to take a stand against current opinion on issues he felt strongly about. He often spoke of his gratitude to his grandfather for teaching him to act according to his belief whatever the consequence might be. There was, however, at least one occasion when he had to learn that this was not always true for a little boy. At the Stambourne chapel it was the custom to repeat the last line of the hymn. So young Charles got it into his head that this must always be done. Later, when back with his parents and worshipping in their chapel, he insisted on repeating the last line of the hymn, whether the rest of the congregation did so or not. He said later, 'It required a great deal of punishment to convince me that a little boy must do what his parents think to be right.'

He left Stambourne with great sadness. Those early years were of greater importance than anyone could possibly have imagined. Looking back on that period of his life he wrote, 'The best point about the old chapel at Stambourne was the blessing which rested on the ministry carried on within. The dew of the Spirit from on high never left the ministry. Wherever my grandfather went, souls were saved under his sermons. When I first of all became a preacher, there were persons who said, 'I heard your grandfather, and I would run my shoes off my feet to hear a Spurgeon.' This was encouraging.

2.
God's hand

There can be no doubt that God's hand was upon young Spurgeon during his formative years. This is highlighted in a remarkable incident that took place in 1844, when he was ten years old. Charles was staying once again at Stambourne and a representative of the London Missionary Society came to speak there. His name was Richard Knill and he was a man with a great desire to see souls saved. From the beginning he took a great interest in the young boy. 'Where do you sleep?' he asked Charles, 'for I want to call you up in the morning.' The following morning at six he came and woke the sleeping boy. The two went out into the garden where Knill spoke warmly and simply to Charles of the love of God. He shared with him some of his missionary experiences and prayed earnestly that Charles would know and serve the Lord. This happened for three successive days and then on the day on which he was to leave, Richard Knill, in the presence of old James Spurgeon and the whole family, took Charles on his knee and said, 'This child will one day preach the gospel, and he will preach it to multitudes. I am persuaded that he will preach in the chapel of Rowland Hill.'

If the ten-year-old was amazed to hear such words, his family were probably even more amazed. They would have known that Rowland Hill, who died the year before Charles was born, was a great preacher whose ministry the Lord had richly blessed. Hill was a controversial character but such was his esteem as a preacher that when George Whitefield died in 1770, he was spoken of as a possible successor. He preached regularly to great crowds and in 1783 Surrey Chapel in London was built especially for him.

To link a young child with such a great preacher was either madness or divine illumination. Richard Knill was no madman. He gave Charles sixpence as a reward for learning the hymn,

> God moves in a mysterious way,
> His wonders to perform,

and made him promise that when he preached in Rowland Hill's chapel, that hymn would be sung. Many years later the prophecy was fulfilled and the promise faithfully kept. Few, if any, of the congregation in Surrey Chapel would have been aware of the significance of the event when the Rev. Charles Spurgeon stood in their pulpit as a last-minute substitute for the expected preacher. But for the preacher it was a highly emotional occasion. He never forgot Richard Knill's words and when he stood once again in the garden at Stambourne in 1887 he walked about the place like one in a dream. He tells us, 'The present minister of Stambourne meeting-house, and the members of his family, including his son and his grandchildren, were in the garden, and I could not help calling them together around the garden, while I praised the Lord for his goodness to me. One irresistible impulse came upon me. It was to pray to God to bless those lads that stood around me. Memory begat prayer. He who blessed me would bless others also. I wanted the lads to remember, when they grew up, my testimony of God's goodness to me. God has blessed me all my life long, and redeemed me from all evil; and I pray that he may be the God of all the young people who read this story.'

Baptism

Believers' baptism was a doctrine which became very precious to Spurgeon, but it was a truth foreign to his religious upbringing. His father and grandfather were both ministers who believed and practised infant baptism. In fact, up until he was fourteen he had not even heard of people called Baptists. Yet Charles was convinced of baptism only for those who had been saved, long before he himself was saved. God's hand was not only guiding him, but the Holy Spirit was teaching him even as an unregenerate teenager. In his autobiography he recalls for us a discussion on the question of baptism that took place a year before he was saved.

'I was about the age of fourteen when I was sent to a Church of England school — now called St Augustine's College, Maidstone.

'One of the clergy was, I believe, a good man, and it is to him I owe that ray of light which sufficed to show me believers' baptism. I was usually at the head of the class, and on one occasion, when the Church of England Catechism was to be repeated, something like the following conversation took place:

Clergyman: "What is your name?"
Spurgeon: "Spurgeon, sir."
C: "No, no; what is your name?"
S: "Charles Spurgeon, sir."
C: "No, you should not behave so, for you know I only want your Christian name."
S: "If you please, sir, I am afraid I haven't got one."
C: "Why, how is that?"
S: "Because I do not think that I am a Christian."
C: "What are you, then — a heathen?"
S: "No, sir; but we may not be heathens, and yet be without the grace of God, and so not be truly Christians."
C: "Well, well, never mind; what is your first name?"
S: "Charles."
C: "Who gave you that name?"
S: "I am sure I don't know, sir; I know no godfathers ever did anything for me, for I never had any. Likely enough, my mother and father did."

C: "Now, you should not set these boys a-laughing. Of course I do not wish you to say the usual answer."

'He seemed always to have respect for me, gave me a copy of *The Christian Year*, in calf leather, as a reward for my great proficiency in religious knowledge.

'Proceeding with the Catechism, he suddenly turned to me, and said, "Spurgeon, you were never properly baptized."
S: "Oh, yes, sir, I was; my grandfather baptized me in the little parlour, and he is a minister, so I know he did it right!"
C: "Ah, but you had neither faith nor repentance, and therefore ought not to have received baptism!"
S: "Why, sir, that has nothing to do with it! All infants ought to be baptized."
C: "How do you know that? Does not the Prayer Book say that faith and repentance are necessary before baptism? And this is so spiritual a doctrine that no one ought to deny it." (Here he went on to show that all the persons spoken of in the Bible as being baptized were believers; which, of course, was an easy task.) "Now, Charles, I shall give you until next week to find whether the Bible does not declare faith and repentance to be necessary qualifications before baptism."

'I felt sure enough of victory; for I thought that a ceremony my grandfather and father both practised in their ministry must be right; but I could not find it — I was beaten — and made up my mind as to the course I would take.

C: "Well, Charles, what do you think now?"
S: "Why, sir, I think you are right, but then it applies to you as well as to me!"
C: "I wanted to show you this; for this is the reason why we appoint sponsors. It is that, without faith, I had no

more right than you to holy baptism, but the promise of my sponsors was accepted by the church as an equivalent. You have no doubt seen your father, when he has no money, give a note of hand for it, and this is regarded as a guarantee of payment, because, as an honest man, we have reason to expect he will honour the note he has given. Now, sponsors are generally good people, and in charity we accept their promise on behalf of the child. As the child cannot at the time have faith, we accept the bond that he will; which promise he fulfils at confirmation, when he takes the bond into his own hands."

S: "Well, sir, I think it is a very bad note of hand."

C: "I have no time to argue that, but I believe it to be good. I will only ask you this: which seems to have the greater regard to Scripture — I, as churchman, or your grandfather as a dissenter? He baptizes in the very teeth of Scripture; and I do not, in my opinion, do so, for I require a promise, which I look upon as an equivalent of repentance and faith, to be rendered in future years."

S: "Really, sir, I think you are more like right; but since it seems to be the truth that only believers should be baptized, I think you are both wrong, though you seem to treat the Bible with greater politeness."

C: "Well, then, you confess that you were not properly baptized; and you would think it your duty, if in your power, to join us, and have sponsors to promise on your behalf."

S: "Oh, no! I have been baptized once, before I ought; I will wait next time till I am fit for it."

C (smiling): "Ah, you are wrong, but I like to see you keep to the Word of God! Seek from him a new heart and divine direction, and you will see one truth after another, and very probably there will be a great change in those opinions which now seem so deeply rooted in you."

'I resolved, from that moment, that if ever divine grace should work a change in me, I would be baptized, since, as I afterwards told my friend the clergyman, "I never ought to be blamed for improper baptism, as I had nothing to do with it; the error, if any, rested with my parents and grandparents.'"

An old cook

God does not always go through the conventional channels when working in the soul of man. Many years later, in his first published book, Spurgeon publicly expressed 'his eternal obligations to an old cook who in her kitchen taught him many of the deep things of God and removed many a doubt from his youthful mind'. The cook's name was Mary King and he came into contact with her towards the end of 1849 when he went to school in Newmarket. She was what Charles called 'a good old soul'. From her he received what he regarded as his first lessons in theology. He said, 'Many a time we have gone over the covenant of grace together, and talked of the personal election of the saints, their union with Christ, their final perseverance, and what vital godliness meant.' It is amazing that such truths were occupying his mind when he was still only fifteen years old, and perhaps even more amazing that his teacher was a school cook. But Mary King was an exceptional woman. 'She lived strongly as well as fed strongly,' and Charles had the highest regard for her. 'The cook at Newmarket was a godly experienced woman, from whom I learnt far more than I did from the minister of the chapel we attended. I asked her once, "Why do you go to such a place?" She replied, "Well, there is no other place of worship to which I can go." I said, "But it must be better to stay at home than to hear such stuff." "Perhaps so," she answered, "but I like to go out to worship even if I get nothing by going. You see a hen scratching all over a heap of rubbish to try to find some corn; she does not get any, but it shows she is looking for it, and using the means to get it, and then, too, the exercise warms her." So the old lady said that scratching over the poor sermon she heard was a blessing to her because it exercised the spiritual faculties and warmed her spirit. On another occasion I told her that I had not found a crumb in the whole sermon, and asked how she fared. "Oh!" she answered, "I got on better tonight, for to all the preacher said, I just put in a *not*, and that turned his talk into real gospel."'

From this cook Charles learnt early in life that 'True seekers will hunt everywhere for Jesus, and will not be too proud to learn from beggars and little children. We take gold from dark mines or muddy streams: it were foolish to refuse instruction in salvation from the most unlettered or uncouth.'

3.
Conviction of sin

God's dealings in the young life of Charles Spurgeon were all for one purpose. He must be convicted of his sin so that he would come in repentance and faith to the Lord Jesus Christ. Some people do not believe that children can be saved. Others believe it is possible, but tend to think of a child's salvation in terms of a simple trust and faith in Jesus, with little or no conviction of sin. That may be the case with some, but it was not that of young Spurgeon. From his own experience he was able to declare, 'As soon as a child is capable of being lost, it is capable of being saved. As soon as a child can sin, that child can, if God's grace assist it, believe and receive the Word of God. As soon as children can learn evil, be assured that they are competent, under the teaching of the Holy Spirit, to learn good.' 'There is no doctrine of the Word of God which a child, if he be capable of salvation, is not capable of receiving. I would have children taught all the great doctrines of truth without a solitary exception.'

His mother's influence

As a young child Charles had heard, and his mind had grappled with, the great truths of Scripture. These truths did their God-ordained work and created in him a very deep conviction of sin. His upbringing had sheltered him from many of the world's worst influences. He considered himself a very respectable young lad who was not dishonest, unfaithful or disobedient, and certainly never swore or broke the Sabbath. The influence of his grandfather and father, who were both ministers, to a great measure ensured this, though, like many boys, he found it difficult to talk to his father on spiritual matters. By far the greatest influence exerted upon him was that of his mother.

On Sunday evenings when his father was preaching, his mother would be at home with the children. She taught them the Scriptures, read to them from children's books and earnestly pleaded for them to God in prayer. One prayer in particular stuck in the mind of Charles: 'Lord, if my children go on in their sins, it will not be from ignorance that they perish, and my soul must bear a swift witness against them at the Day of Judgement if they lay not hold of Christ.' The thought of his mother bearing witness against him pierced his conscience and was probably the beginning of a real awareness of his need of salvation.

In his early youth no teaching made such an impression upon him as the instruction of his mother. The seriousness with which Elizabeth Spurgeon took her spiritual responsibilities as a mother is highlighted in the following incident: 'Well do I remember hearing my father speak of an incident that greatly impressed him. He used to be frequently away from home preaching, and at one time, as he was on his way to a service, he feared that he was neglecting his own family while caring for the souls of others. He therefore turned back, and went to his home. On arriving there, he was surprised to find no one in the lower rooms of the house but on ascending the stairs, he heard the sound as of someone engaged in prayer. On listening at the bedroom door, he discovered that it was my mother, pleading most earnestly for the salvation of all her children, and specially praying for Charles, her first-born and strong-willed son. My father felt that he might safely go about his Master's business while his dear wife was caring so well

for the spiritual interests of the boys and girls at home, so he
did not disturb her, but proceeded at once to fulfil his preaching engagement.'

Growing conviction

The prayers of his godly mother were heard and as Charles
reached the age of ten a growing conviction of sin was
developing in him. One of its first effects was to shatter the
illusion that he could turn to God whenever he pleased.
Powerful sermons shook him and he tried to pray for forgive-
ness, but it seemed impossible. 'How hard,' he said, 'is
prevailing prayer to a poor God-provoking sinner!' His
thoughts of his own respectability were also shattered when 'I
met Moses carrying in his hand the law of God, and as he
looked at me, he seemed to search me through and through
with his eyes of fire. He bade me read "God's Ten Words" —
the Ten Commandments — and as I read them, they all seemed
to join in accusing and condemning me in the sight of the
thrice-holy Jehovah. When I saw myself in this condition, I
could say nothing in self-defence, or by way of excuse. I
confessed my transgression in solemn silence unto the Lord,
but I could speak no word of self-justification, or apology, for
I felt that I was verily guilty of grievous sins against the Holy
One of Israel. At that time, a dreadful silence reigned within
my spirit; even if I had tried to say a word in my own favour,
I should have been self-condemned as a liar.'

These strivings of the Holy Spirit in the heart of a young boy
are not to be despised or dismissed lightly. They may not be the
experience of every boy, but they certainly were that of
Charles Spurgeon. The old fear of the bottomless pit came
back to him, and night after night he dreamed of this. 'For five
years, as a child, there was nothing before my eyes but my
guilt, and though I do not hesitate to say that those who
observed my life would not have seen any extraordinary sin,
yet as I looked upon myself, there was not a day in which I did

not commit such gross, such outrageous sins against God, that often I wished I had never been born.'

In these days of pop evangelism and a 'Smile, Jesus loves you' gospel, such depths of conviction in a young boy are almost unbelievable. Some would even say they are unhealthy. How do we explain God's dealing with this particular youngster? Spurgeon supplies his own explanation: 'I do think it often proves a great blessing to a man that he had a terrible conflict, a desperate encounter, a hard-fought engagement in passing from the empire of Satan into the kingdom of God's dear Son. Sooner or later, each saved man will have his hand-to-hand fight with the prince of darkness, and, as a general rule, it is a great mercy to have it over at the outset of one's career, and to be able afterwards to feel, whatever comes upon me, I never can suffer as I suffered when I was seeking Christ. I do not say that it is desirable that we should seek it as an evidence of regeneration, but when we have passed through it victoriously, we may so use it that it may be a perpetual armoury to us. If we can now defy all doubts and fears that come, because they cannot be so potent as those that already, in the name of Jesus Christ our Saviour, we have overthrown, shall we not use that fact for ourselves, and can we not equally well use it for others? Full often have I found it good, when I have talked with a young convert in deep distress about his sin, to tell him something more of his anxious plight than he knew how to express, and he has wondered where I found it, though he would not have wondered if he had known where I had been, and how much deeper in the mire than he. When he has talked about some horrible thought that he has had, with regard to the impossibility of his own salvation, I have said, "Why, I have thought that a thousand times, and yet have overcome it through the help of God's Spirit!" I know that a man's experience is one of the very best weapons he can use in fighting with the evil in other men's hearts. Often, their misery and despondency, aggravated, as it commonly is, by a feeling of solitariness, will be greatly relieved before it is effectually driven out when they find that a brother has suffered the same,

and yet has been able to overcome. Do I show him how
precious the Saviour is to my soul? He glorifies God in me.
Right soon will he look into the same dear face and be
lightened, and then he will magnify the Lord with me, and we
shall exalt his name together.'

Light

With the darkness of conviction came a faint but growing ray
of light. Charles began to have an overwhelming sense of
God's greatness, majesty and holiness. This led inevitably to
a greater awareness of sin, but also to a greater longing for
salvation. He was caused to cry to God, 'Oh, that I had a part
and lot in such a salvation as that!' by words of hymns such as,

My name from the palm of his hands
Eternity will not erase;
Impressed on his heart it remains
In marks of indelible grace;
Yes, I to the end shall endure,
As sure as the earnest is given;
More happy, but not more secure,
The glorified spirits in heaven.

Before he was saved he knew that if God would save him,
then it would be a salvation for all eternity. To this boy seeking
God, the enchanting part of the gospel was the knowledge that
if God would love him, he would keep him to the end. This
made the gospel more precious and his longing for salvation
more earnest.

This longing for God was no passing teenage emotion, but
something that dominated the life of young Spurgeon for
years. As with many in a similar condition, he began to wonder
if God would ever save him. 'I recollect the time when I was
afraid that Jesus would never save me, but I used to feel in my
heart that, even if he did not, I must love him for what he had

done for other poor sinners. From chapel to chapel I went to hear the Word preached, but never a gospel sentence did I hear, but this one text preserved me from what I believe I should have been driven to—the commission of suicide through grief and sorrow. It was this sweet word, "Whosoever shall call upon the name of the Lord shall be saved." Well, I thought, I cannot believe on Christ as I could wish, I cannot find pardon, but I know I call upon his name, I know I pray, and pray with groans, and tears, and sighs, day and night; and if I am lost, I will plead that promise, "O God, thou saidst, 'Whosoever shall call upon my name shall be saved!' I did call; wilt thou cast me away? I did plead thy promise; I did lift up my heart in prayer; canst thou be just, and yet condemn the sinner who really did call upon thy name?"

'My heart was greatly impressed by something I heard my mother say. I had been some years seeking Christ, and I could not believe that he would save me. She said she had heard many people swear and blaspheme God, but one thing she had never known — she had never heard a man say he had sought Christ, and Christ had rejected him. I thought that I could say it; I thought I had sought him, and he had cast me away, and I determined that I would say it; even if it destroyed my soul, I would seek what I thought was the truth. But I said to myself, "I will try once more," and I went to the Master, with nothing of my own, casting myself simply on his mercy; and I believed that he died for me, and now, blessed be his holy name, I never shall be able to say that he has cast me away! As the result of personal experience, I can add my own testimony to that of my mother.'

There can be no doubt that Charles was no ordinary teenager. With a father and grandfather who were ministers, he would be expected to have a knowledge of Scripture, but his knowledge was not merely superficial. His interest in, and his grasp of, doctrine was exceptional. His enquiring mind would not allow him to be satisfied with just a surface knowledge. He had to know the meaning. It is always a danger that youngsters from Christian homes can supply all the correct answers to biblical truths. Spurgeon had head knowledge and also heart knowledge; what he lacked was heart experience of what the Scriptures taught of salvation. He certainly had knowledge in his heart of the reality of sin and the wrath of God. Bible truths never rested idly in his mind alone; they shook his heart and conscience. But it was not until that snowy Sunday morning in Colchester that the full glory and simplicity of biblical truth invaded his experience and he became a Christian.

4.
Conversion

God's dealing with a soul in salvation is such a personal and intimate matter that for us to understand it fully we must if possible allow the individual to speak for himself. So here, then, is Charles Spurgeon's own account of his conversion.

'When I was in the hand of the Holy Spirit, under conviction of sin, I had a clear and sharp sense of the justice of God. Sin, whatever it might be to other people, became to me an intolerable burden. It was not so much that I feared hell, as that I feared sin; and all the while, I had upon my mind a deep concern for the honour of God's name, and the integrity of his moral government. I felt that it would not satisfy my conscience if I could be forgiven unjustly. But then there came the question: "How could God be just, and yet justify me who had been so guilty?" I was worried and wearied with this question; neither could I see any answer to it. Certainly, I could never have invented an answer which would have satisfied my conscience. The doctrine of the atonement is to my mind one of the surest proofs of the divine inspiration of Holy Scripture. Who would or could have thought of the just ruler dying for the unjust rebel? This is no teaching of human mythology, or dream of poetical imagination. This method of expiation is only known among men because it is a fact: fiction could not have devised it. God himself ordained it; it is not a matter which could have been imagined.

'I had heard of the plan of salvation by the sacrifice of Jesus from my youth up; but I did not know any more about it in my innermost soul than if I had been born and bred a heathen. The light was there, but I was blind: it was of necessity that the Lord himself should make the matter plain to me. It came to me as a new revelation, as fresh as if I had never read in Scripture that Jesus was declared to be the propitiation for sins, that God might be just. I believe it will have to come as a revelation to every new-born child of God whenever he sees it; I mean that glorious doctrine of the substitution of the Lord Jesus...

'When I was anxious about the possibility of a just God pardoning me, I understood and saw by faith that he who is the Son of God became man, and in his own person bore my sin in his own body on the tree. I saw that the chastisement of my peace was laid on him, and that with his stripes I was healed. It was because the Son of God, supremely glorious in his matchless person, undertook to vindicate the law by bearing the sentence due to me, that therefore God was able to pass by my sin. My sole hope for heaven lies in the full atonement made upon Calvary's cross for the ungodly. On that I firmly rely. I have not the shadow of a hope anywhere else. Personally, I could never have overcome my own sinfulness. I tried and failed. My evil tendencies were too many for me, till, in the belief that Christ died for me, I cast my guilty soul on him, and then I received a conquering principle by which I overcame my sinful self.

'In my conversion, the very point lay in making the discovery that I had nothing to do but to look at Christ, and I should be saved. I believe that I had been a very good, attentive hearer; my own impression about myself was that nobody ever listened much better than I did. For years, as a child, I tried to learn the way of salvation, and either I did not hear it set forth, which I think cannot quite be the case, or else I was spiritually blind and deaf, and could not see it and could not hear it; but the good news that I was, as a sinner, to look away from myself to Christ, as much startled me ... as any news I ever heard in my life. Had I never been taught by Christian people? Yes, I had, by mother and father and others. Had I not heard the gospel? Yes, I think I had; and yet somehow, it was like a new revelation to me that I was to "believe and live". I confess to have been tutored in piety, put into my cradle by prayerful hands, and lulled to sleep by songs concerning Jesus, but after having heard the gospel continually, with line upon line, precept upon precept, here much and there much, yet when the Word of the Lord came to me with power, it was as new as if I had lived among the unvisited tribes of central Africa, and had never heard the tidings of the cleansing fountain filled with blood, drawn from the Saviour's veins.

'When, for the first time, I received the gospel to my soul's salvation, I thought that I never had really heard it before, and I began to think that the preachers to whom I had listened had not truly preached it. But, on looking back, I am inclined to believe that I had heard the gospel fully preached many hundreds of times before, and that this was the difference — that I then heard it as though I heard it not; and when I did hear it, the message may not have been any more clear in itself than it had been in former times, but the power of the Holy Spirit was present to open my ear, and guide the message to my heart. I have no doubt that I heard, scores of times, such texts as these: "He that believeth and is baptized shall be saved"; "Look unto me, and be ye saved, all the ends of the earth", "As Moses lifted up the serpent in the wilderness, even so must the Son of man be lifted up: that whosoever believeth in him should not perish, but have everlasting life; yet I had no intelligent idea of what faith meant. When I first discovered what faith really was, and exercised it — for with me these two things came together, I believed as soon as ever I knew what believing meant — then I thought I had never heard before the truth preached. But, now, I am persuaded that the light shone often on my eyes, but I was blind, and therefore I thought that the light had never come there. The light was shining all the while, but there was no power to receive it; the eyeball of the soul was not sensitive to the divine beams.

'Personally, I have to bless God for many good books; I

thank him for Dr Doddridge's *Rise and Progress of Religion in the Soul*, for Baxter's *Call to the Unconverted*, for Alleine's *Alarm to Unconverted Sinners,* and for James' *Anxious Enquirer*, but my gratitude most of all is due to God, not for books, but for the preached Word — and that too addressed to me by a poor, uneducated man, a man who had never received any training for the ministry, and probably will never be heard of in this life, a man engaged in business, no doubt of a humble kind, during the week, but who had just enough grace to say on the Sabbath, "Look unto me, and be ye saved, all the ends of the earth." The books were good, but the man was better. The revealed Word awakened me, but it was the preached Word that saved me; and I must ever attach peculiar value to the hearing of the truth, for by it I received the joy and peace in which my soul delights. While under concern of soul, I resolved that I would attend all the places of worship in the town where I lived, in order that I might find out the way of salvation. I was willing to do anything, and be anything, if God would only forgive my sin. I set off, determined to go round all the chapels, and I did go to every place of worship; but for a long time I went in vain. I do not, however, blame the ministers. One man preached divine sovereignty; I could hear him with pleasure, but what was that sublime truth to a poor sinner who wished to know what he must do to be saved? There was another admirable man who always preached about the law, but what was the use of ploughing up ground that needed to be sown? Another was a practical preacher. I heard him, but it was very much like a commanding officer teaching the manoeuvres of war to a set of men without feet. What could I do? All his exhortations were lost on me. I know it was said, "Believe on the Lord Jesus Christ, and thou shalt be saved," but I did not know what it was to believe on Christ. These good men all preached truths suited to many in their congregations who were spiritually-minded people, but what I wanted to know was, "How can I get my sins forgiven?" — and they never told me that. I desired to hear how a poor sinner, under a sense of sin, might find peace with God.

'I sometimes think I might have been in darkness and despair until now had it not been for the goodness of God in sending a snowstorm, one Sunday morning, while I was going to a certain place of worship. When I could go no further, I turned down a side street, and came to a little Primitive Methodist Chapel. In that chapel there may have been a dozen or fifteen people. I had heard of the Primitive Methodists, how they sang so loudly that they made people's heads ache; but that did not matter to me. I wanted to know how I might be saved, and if they could tell me that, I did not care how much they made my head ache. The minister did not come that morning; he was snowed up, I suppose. At last, a very thin-looking man, a shoemaker, or tailor, or something of that sort, went up into the pulpit to preach. Now, it is well that preachers should be instructed, but this man was really stupid. He was obliged to stick to his text, for the simple reason that he had little else to say.

'The text was, "Look unto me, and be ye saved, all the ends of the earth." He did not even pronounce the words rightly, but that did not matter. There was, I thought, a glimpse of hope for me in that text. The preacher began thus: "My dear friends, this is a very simple text indeed. It says, 'Look'. Now lookin' don't take a deal of pain. It ain't liftin' your foot or your finger; it is just, 'Look'. Well, a man needn't go to college to learn to look. You may be the biggest fool, and yet you can look... Anyone can look; even a child can look. But then the text says, 'Look unto me.' Ay!" said he, in broad Essex, "many on ye are lookin' to yourselves, but it's no use lookin' there. You'll never find any comfort in yourselves. Some look to God the Father. No, look to him by and by. Jesus Christ says, 'Look unto me.' Some on ye say, 'We must wait for the Spirit's workin'.' You have no business with that just now. Look to Christ. The text says, 'Look unto me.'" Then the good man followed up his text in this way: "Look unto me; I am sweatin' great drops of blood. Look unto me; I am hangin' on the cross. Look unto me; I am dead and buried. Look unto me; I rise again. Look unto me; I ascend to heaven. Look unto me; I am

The Primitive Methodist Chapel, Colchester

sittin' at the Father's right hand. O poor sinner, look unto me! Look unto me!"

'When he had gone to about that length and managed to spin out ten minutes or so, he was at the end of his tether. Then he looked at me under the gallery, and I dare say, with so few present, he knew me to be a stranger. Just fixing his eyes on me, as if he knew all my heart, he said, "Young man, you look very miserable." Well, I did, but I had not been accustomed to have remarks made from the pulpit on my personal appearance before. However, it was a good blow, struck right home. He continued, "And you always will be miserable — miserable in life, and miserable in death — if you don't obey my text; but if you obey now, this moment you will be saved." Then, lifting up his hands, he shouted, as only a Primitive Methodist can do, "Young man, look to Jesus Christ. Look! Look! Look! You have nothin' to do but to look and live." I saw at once the way of salvation. I know not what else he said — I did not take much notice of it — I was so possessed with that one thought. Like as when the brazen serpent was lifted up, the people only looked and were healed, so it was with me. I had been waiting to do fifty things, but when I heard that word, "Look!" what a charming word it seemed to me! Oh! I looked until I could almost have looked my eyes away. There and then the cloud was gone, the darkness had rolled away, and that moment I saw the sun; and I could have risen that instant, and sung with the most enthusiastic of them, of the precious blood of Christ, and the simple faith which looks alone to him. Oh, that somebody had told me this before, "Trust Christ, and you shall be saved." Yet it was, no doubt, all wisely ordered, and now I can say,

> E'er since by faith I saw the stream
> Thy flowing wounds supply,
> Redeeming love has been my theme,
> And shall be till I die.

'Since that dear moment when my soul cast itself on Jesus, I have found solid joy and peace; but before that, all those

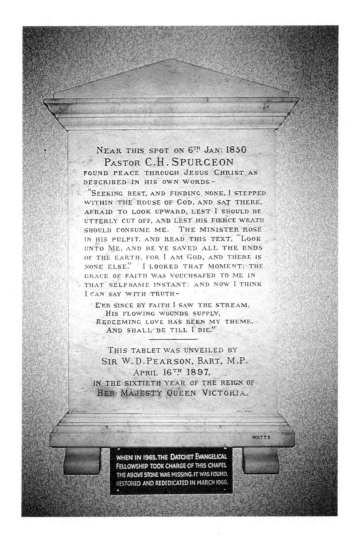

Commemorative plaque indicating the seat where Spurgeon
was converted

supposed gaieties of early youth, all the imagined ease and joy of boyhood, were but vanity and vexation of spirit to me. That happy day, when I found the Saviour, and learned to cling to his dear feet, was a day never to be forgotten by me. An obscure child, unknown, unheard of, I listened to the Word of God; and that precious text led me to the cross of Christ. I can testify that the joy of that day was utterly indescribable. I could have leaped; I could have danced; there was no expression, however, which would have been out of keeping with the joy of my spirit at that hour. Many days of Christian experience have passed since then, but there has never been one which has had the full exhilaration, the sparkling delight which that first day had. I thought I could have sprung from the seat on which I sat, and have called out with the wildest of those Methodist brethren who were present, "I am forgiven! I am forgiven! A monument of grace! A sinner saved by blood!" My spirit saw its chains broken to pieces, I felt that I was an emancipated soul, an heir of heaven, a forgiven one, accepted in Christ Jesus, plucked out of the miry clay and out of the horrible pit, with my feet set upon a rock, and my goings established. I thought I could dance all the way home. I could understand what John Bunyan meant when he declared he wanted to tell the crows on the ploughed land all about his conversion. He was too full to hold; he felt he must tell somebody.

'Between half-past ten o'clock, when I entered the chapel, and half-past twelve o'clock, when I was back again at home, what a change had taken place in me! I had passed from darkness into marvellous light, from death to life. Simply by looking to Jesus, I had been delivered from despair, and I was brought into such a joyous state of mind that, when they saw me at home they said to me, "Something wonderful has happened to you," and I was eager to tell them all about it. Oh, there was joy in the household that day, when all heard that the eldest son had found the Saviour, and knew himself to be forgiven — bliss compared with which all earth's joys are less than nothing, and vanity! Yes, I had looked to Jesus as I was, and found in him my Saviour. Thus had the eternal purpose of

Jehovah decreed it; and as, the moment before, there was none more wretched than I was, so within that second, there was none more joyous. It took no longer time than does the lightning-flash; it was done, and never has it been undone. I looked, and lived, and leaped in joyful liberty as I beheld my sin punished upon the great substitute, and put away for ever. I looked unto him, as he bled upon that tree; his eyes darted a glance of love unutterable into my spirit and, in a moment, I was saved.

'The frown of God no longer resteth upon me; but my Father smiles. I see his eyes — they are glancing love; I hear his voice — it is full of sweetness. I am forgiven, I am forgiven, I am forgiven!

'When I look back upon it, I can see one reason why the Word was blessed to me as I heard it preached in that Primitive Methodist Chapel at Colchester; I had been up early crying to God for the blessing. As a lad, when I was seeking the Saviour, I used to rise with the sun, that I might get time to read gracious books, and to seek the Lord. I can recall the kind of pleas I used when I took my arguments, and came before the throne of grace: "Lord, save me; it will glorify thy grace to save such a sinner as I am! Lord, else I am lost to all eternity; do not let me perish, Lord! Save me, O Lord, for Jesus died! By his agony and bloody sweat, by his cross and passion, save me!" I often proved that the early morning was the best part of the day; I liked those prayers of which the psalmist said, "In the morning shall my prayer prevent thee."

'The Holy Sprit, who enabled me to believe, gave me peace through believing. I felt as sure that I was forgiven as before I felt sure of condemnation. I had been certain of my condemnation because the Word of God declared it, and my conscience bore witness to it, but when the Lord justified me, I was made equally certain by the same witness. The Word of the Lord in the Scripture saith, "He that believeth on him is not condemned," and my conscience bore witness that I believed, and that God in pardoning me was just. Thus I had the witness of the Holy Spirit and also of my own conscience, and these two agreed in one.

'Has Jesus saved me? I dare not speak with any hesitation here; I know he has. His Word is true; therefore I am saved. My evidence that I am saved does not lie in the fact that I preach, or that I do this or that. All my hope lies in this, that Jesus Christ came to save sinners. I am a sinner; I trust him; then he came to save me, and I am saved. I live habitually in the enjoyment of this blessed fact, and it is long since I have doubted the truth of it, for I have his own Word to sustain my faith. It is a very surprising thing — a thing to be marvelled at most of all by those who enjoy it. I know that it is to me even to this day the greatest wonder that I ever heard of that God should ever justify me. I feel myself to be a lump of unworthiness, a mass of corruption, and a heap of sin, apart from his almighty love; yet I know, by a full assurance, that I am justified by faith which is in Christ Jesus, and treated as if I had been perfectly just, and made an heir of God and a joint-heir with Christ; though by nature I must take my place among the most sinful. I, who am altogether undeserving, am treated as if I had been deserving. I am loved with as much love as if I had always been godly, whereas aforetime I was ungodly.'

5.
Experiences after conversion

The joy and excitement of conversion can last for days, weeks or even months before the realities of the spiritual battle and the Christian warfare make themselves known. With Charles it was only five days before despondency attacked him. The cause was typical of a young convert. He thought that now he was a Christian, he was finished with sin. The devil would never again be able to tempt him or lead him astray. How many young believers have thought the same, only to be rudely awakened by what Spurgeon called 'an intruder ... an evil heart of unbelief'! He could not live without sinning.

His answer to the problem was to go back the next Sunday to the church in which he was converted. To his joy the text of the sermon seemed to be just what he needed: 'O wretched man that I am! who shall deliver me from the body of this death?' (Rom. 7:24). Unfortunately the preacher began by saying that Paul was not a believer when he said that. He went on to say that no Christian ever felt such a conflict within. This was no help to a new Christian like Charles, but he had the good sense to realize how wrong that exposition was, 'So I took up my hat, and left the chapel, and I have very seldom attended such places since. They are very good for people who are unconverted to go to, but of very little use for children of God.'

He discovered that conviction of sin is not only a necessary

prelude to salvation, but after conversion it continues to haunt
the Christian with even greater ferocity. 'I thought the sins I
knew before, though they were cruel task-masters, were not
half so much to be dreaded as those soldier sins, armed with
spears and axes ... hastening to assault me. It is true, they did
not come so near me as before; nevertheless they occasioned
me more fright even than when I was their slave.'

For instance, his family upbringing had sheltered him from
much sin and he had hardly ever heard a man swear. 'Yet I do
remember times in my earliest Christian days, when there
came into my mind thoughts so evil that I clapped my hands
to my mouth for fear I should be led to give utterance to them.
This is one way in which Satan tortures those whom God has
delivered out of his hand. Many of the choicest saints have
been thus molested. Once, when I had been grievously assailed by the tempter, I went to see my dear grandfather. I told
him about my terrible experience, and then I wound up by
saying, "Grandfather, I am sure I cannot be a child of God, or
else I should never have such evil thoughts as these." "Non-
sense, Charles," answered the good old man; "it is just because
you are a Christian that you are thus tempted. These blas-
phemies are no children of yours; they are the devil's brats,
which he delights to lay at the door of a Christian. Do not own
them as yours, give them neither house room nor heart room."
I felt greatly comforted by what my grandfather said.'

Mistakes

The mistakes of the new convert are sometimes the results of
ignorance and often the result of misguided enthusiasm.
Charles Spurgeon at fifteen was a great enthusiast, determined
to serve his Lord well. This determination led him to make
rules as to when he would pray, how long he would pray, and
even how many people and subjects he would pray for. He
soon learnt that such rules strangle rather than help prayer, and
his rule-book of spiritual life was soon dispensed with in

favour of a more biblical pattern. From this mistake of enthusiasm, one benefit did stay with him. That was the habit of regular morning and evening prayer which he considered indispensable to a believer's life.

The Bible encourages self-examination, but Charles took this further than God intends. He caused himself much pain and heartache by continually looking for signs, marks and evidences in his life, instead of keeping his eye on the Lord Jesus Christ. For instance, by way of self-examination, he would sometimes ask himself, 'Am I afraid to die?' Often the honest answer was that, yes, he was afraid to die. His conclusion then was that if that was the case he could not be a Christian. So doubts and lack of assurance were self-imposed.

He was greatly helped in this matter by a sermon his grandfather preached on the text, 'The God of all grace'. He never forgot that sermon. 'He interested the assembly, after describing the different kinds of grace that God gave, by saying at the end of each period, "But there is one kind of grace that you do not want." After each part of this theme, there came the sentence, "But there is one kind of grace you do not want." And then he wound up by saying, "You don't want dying grace in living moments, but you shall have grace when you need it. When you are in the condition to require it, you shall have grace enough if you put your trust in Christ."'

Encouragements

Older Christians can be a great help and encouragement to the new convert. Charles heard a preacher who was eighty years old and had been blind for twenty years. This old saint spoke with warmth and passion of his fifty-six years as a Christian. His love for the Lord was so obvious, and his experience of Christ so real, that young Spurgeon's own heart leapt in delight. He said of this old preacher, 'His testimony was such as a younger man could not have borne; he might have spoken more fluently, but the weight of those eighty years at the back of it made the old man eloquent to my young heart. For twenty years he had not seen the light of the sun. There stood the dear old man, tottering into his tomb, deprived of the light of heaven naturally, and yet having the light of heaven in a better sense shining into his soul; and though he could not look upon us, yet he turned towards us, and he seemed to say, "Young people, trust God early in life, for I have not lived to regret that I have sought him too soon. I have only to mourn that so many of my years ran to waste." There is nothing that more tends to strengthen the faith of the young believer than to hear the veteran Christian covered with scars from the battle, testifying that the service of his Master is a happy service, and that if he could have served any other master, he would not have done so, for his service is pleasant, and his reward everlasting joy.'

Perhaps the greatest encouragement that Charles found was in the Word of God. He had been accustomed to reading Scripture for many years, and he had learned to appreciate its language and beauty. But when he was saved the Bible became a new book to him. All through his life Charles had a tendency to despondency, but the Bible was always to him a source of joy and intense pleasure. It showed him his weaknesses and how to deal with them. Above all, it showed him the Lord Jesus Christ, and that to Spurgeon was always the best sight. All Christians find that certain verses of Scripture speak to them more powerfully than others.

As a young believer, one verse was most precious to Charles. It was often in his mind and on his lips. It was Psalm 118:27: 'Bind the sacrifice with cords, even unto the horns of the altar.' It may seem a strange verse to so impress itself upon a teenage Christian, but to Charles it gave a personal assurance of wholly belonging to Christ. Many years later, he wrote of this verse, 'We are bound to Christ himself, who is both altar and sacrifice. We desire to be more bound to him than ever. Our soul finds her liberty in being tethered fast to the altar of the Lord.' The young Spurgeon would not have been able to have written such words, but something of the experience they convey was being born in his heart even as a teenager.

6.
Baptism

Charles was now very anxious to become a member of the Congregational Church at Newmarket. He wanted membership because, 'I felt that I could not be happy without fellowship with the people of God. I wanted to be wherever they were, and if anyone ridiculed them, I wished to be ridiculed with them; if any people had an ugly name for them, I wanted to be called by that ugly name, for I felt that, unless I suffered with Christ in his humiliation, I could not expect to reign with him in his glory.'

This commendable desire was not easily fulfilled. On four successive days he called to see the minister, but for some reason or other an interview was not possible. Not to be put off, he wrote to the minister and told him that he would go to the church meeting and propose himself as a member. The minister had probably never been confronted by such determination before. Whether or not Spurgeon actually had to resort to the drastic measure he had proposed, we don't know; but he was very soon accepted as a member.

Baptist convictions

He was now invited to the communion table but he refused, because he was convinced that he should first be baptized as a believer. So his next objective was baptism. We have seen that his father and grandfather, as ministers of the gospel, both practised infant baptism. However for some time, Charles had been unhappy with this, but still he was a young man with a deep respect for his parents.

On 6 April 1850 he wrote to his father, 'My dear father, You will be pleased to hear that, last Thursday night, I was admitted as a member. Oh, that I may henceforth live more for the glory of him by whom I feel assured that I shall be everlastingly saved! Owing to my scruples on account of baptism, I did not sit down at the Lord's table, and cannot in conscience do so until I am baptized. To one who does not see the necessity of baptism, it is perfectly right and proper to partake of this blessed privilege; but were I to do so, I conceive would be to tumble over the wall, since I feel persuaded it is Christ's appointed way of professing him. I am sure this is the only view which I have of baptism. I detest the idea that I can do a single thing towards my own salvation. I trust that I feel sufficiently the corruption of my heart to know that, instead of doing one iota to forward my own salvation, my own corrupt heart would impede it, were it not that my Redeemer is mighty, and works as he pleases.'

He concluded that letter: 'As Mr Cantlow's baptizing season will come round this month, I have humbly to beg your consent, as I will not act against your will, and should very much like to commune next month. I have no doubt of your permission. We are all one in Christ; forms and ceremonies, I trust, will not make us divided.'

His father was slow in answering, and so Charles with his usual impatience wrote to his mother on 20 April: 'My dear mother, I have every morning looked for a letter from father. I long for an answer; it is now a month since I have had one from him. Do, if you please, send me either permission or refusal to be baptized; I have been kept in painful suspense. This is the 20th, and Mr Cantlow's baptizing day is to the latter end of the month; I think, next week. I should be so sorry to lose another ordinance Sunday; and with my present convictions,

I hope I shall never so violate my conscience as to sit down unbaptized. When requested, I assured the members at the church meeting that I would never do so.'

The longed-for letter arrived on 25 April, but it was not altogether to Charles' liking. He wrote in his diary for that day, 'A letter from father: in truth, he is rather hard upon me.' It appears that John Spurgeon did not refuse his son permission to be baptized, but he expressed certain fears. Charles refers to these in the entry in his diary for the following day: 'How my father's fears that I should trust to baptism stir up my soul! My God, thou knowest that I hate such a thought.' Obviously, he was very upset by his father's letter, but permission was granted.

His soul was not stirred up for too long, and on another occasion he was able to joke with his mother on the subject: 'My mother said to me, one day, "Ah, Charles! I often prayed to the Lord to make you a Christian, but I never asked that you might become a Baptist." I could not resist the temptation to reply, "Ah, mother! the Lord has answered your prayer with his usual bounty, and given exceedingly abundantly above what you asked or thought."'

It was no small thing for a fifteen-year-old to take such a stand. He recounts for us his feelings at the time: 'I had attended the house of God with my father, and my grandfather, but I thought, when I read the Scriptures, that it was my business to judge for myself. I knew that my father and my grandfather took little children in their arms, put a few drops of water on their faces, and said they were baptized. But I could not see anything in my Bible about babes being baptized. I learned a little Greek, but I could not discover that the word "baptize" meant to sprinkle, so I said to myself, "They are good men, yet they may be wrong; and though I love and revere them, that is no reason why I should imitate them." And they acknowledged, when they knew of my honest conviction, that it was quite right for me to act according to my conscience. I consider the "baptism" of an unconscious infant is just as foolish as the "baptism" of a ship or a bell, for there is as much

Scripture for the one as for the other. Therefore, I left my relations, and became what I am today, a Baptist, so called, but I hope a great deal more a Christian than a Baptist.

'When I was fifteen, I believed in the Lord Jesus, was baptized, and joined the church of Christ, and nothing upon earth would please me more than to hear of other boys having been led to do the same. I have never been sorry for what I did then: no, not even once.'

Baptized

Many obstacles seemed to conspire to prevent Charles from realizing his great desire for believers' baptism. Not the least was the fact that he was now a member of a Congregational church, whose views on baptism were the same as his father's. So he looked around for a Baptist minister. The nearest one was a Mr W. W. Cantlow of Isleham, eight miles away. The date was set for 3 May 1850, which happened to be Mrs Spurgeon's birthday, and a few weeks short of Charles' own birthday.

The 3rd of May was a weekday, but Charles was granted a day's holiday by his employer. He was up very early that morning in order to spend a few hours in prayer. Then there followed the two or three-hour walk to Isleham. The baptism was to take place at Isleham Ferry, on the Lark, about half a mile outside the village. It was a cold day and Mr Cantlow was waiting for him by a peat-fire on the riverbank. Baptists of that day scorned the comfort of an indoor baptistry and warm water. The River Lark is not very wide and served as an ideal baptistry; in fact over a stretch of seven or eight miles, no less than five Baptist churches used it.

On a Sunday great crowds would gather at a baptism but on weekdays the spectators were normally few. This did not bother Charles. In fact, he says, 'To me, there seemed to be a great concourse on that weekday. Dressed, I believe, in a jacket with a boy's turn-down collar, I attended the service

Isleham Ferry, where Spurgeon was baptized

previous to the ordinance but all remembrance of it has gone from me: my thoughts were in the water, sometimes with my Lord in joy, and sometimes with myself in trembling awe at making so public a confession. There were first to be baptized two women — Diana Wilkinson and Eunice Fuller — and I was asked to conduct them through the water to the minister, but this I most timidly declined. It was a new experience to me, never having seen a baptism before, and I was afraid of making some mistake. The wind blew down the river with a cutting blast, and my turn came to wade into the flood, but after I had walked a few steps, and noted the people on the ferryboat and in boats and on either shore, I felt as if heaven and earth and hell might all gaze upon me, for I was not ashamed, there and then, to own myself a follower of the Lamb. My timidity was washed away; it floated down the river into the sea and must have been devoured by the fishes, for I have not felt anything of the kind since. Baptism also loosed my tongue, and from that day it has never been quiet. I lost a thousand fears in the River Lark, and found that "In keeping his commandments there is a great reward." It was a thrice happy day to me. God be praised for the preserving goodness which allows me to write of it with delight so long afterwards!'

Why was the fifteen-year-old so determined to be baptized? He had never seen a baptism and he had probably never heard a Baptist preach on the subject. There was no undue pressure upon him from some strong-willed older believer. In fact, it was quite the opposite. It seems it was simply a result of how this young man read and understood the Scriptures. He said, 'If you ask, why was I thus baptized, I answer, because I believed it to be an ordinance of Christ, very specially joined by him. I had no superstitious idea that baptism would save me, for I was saved. I did not seek to have sin washed away by water, for I believed that my sins were forgiven me through faith in Jesus Christ. Yet I regarded baptism as the token to the believer of cleansing, the emblem of his burial with his Lord, and the outward avowal of his new birth. I did not trust in it; but, because I trusted in Jesus as my Saviour, I felt bound to obey him as my Lord, and follow the example which he set us in Jordan, in his own baptism. I did not fulfil the outward ordinance to join a party, and to become a Baptist, but to become a Christian after the apostolic fashion, for they, when they believed, were baptized.'

7.
Serving the Lord

Charles was now saved, a member of the church and baptized. To some Christians that is the sum total of their spiritual experience, but not for this young man. He had a great longing to serve his Lord and to win other souls for Christ. Like many other young converts, he had more enthusiasm than wisdom. As a result, many of his first activities were unwise, but there are few things more exciting than to see the unbridled zeal of the new convert. He would write texts on scraps of paper and drop them everywhere in the hope that someone would pick them up and read them. 'I could scarcely content myself even for five minutes without trying to do something for Christ. If I walked along the street, I must have a few tracts with me: if I went into a railway carriage, I must drop a tract out of a window.' It is easy to frown in disapproval of such activities, but this was the product of a heart on fire for the Lord. Young Spurgeon had no thought of being a preacher, so he did what he was able to do. His only free time was on Saturday afternoons and this he gave to tract work. 'The very first service which my youthful heart rendered to Christ was the placing of tracts in envelopes, and then sealing them up, that I might send them, with the hope that, by choosing suitable tracts, applicable to persons I knew, God would bless them. And I well remember taking tracts, and distributing them in certain districts in the town of Newmarket, going from house to house, and telling, in humble language, the things of the kingdom of God. I might have done nothing for Christ if I had not been encouraged by finding myself able to do a little. Then I sought to do something more, and from that something more, and I do not doubt that many of the servants of God have been led on to higher and nobler labours for their Lord, because they began to serve him in the right spirit and manner. I look upon the giving away of a religious tract as only the first step. We might never reach to the second; but that being attained, we are encouraged to take the next, and so, at the last, God helping us, we may be made extensively useful.'

Sunday School teacher

It was not long before Charles was asked to teach a Sunday School class. He was not very anxious to do this, but felt he could not refuse. It was a rather fearful Spurgeon who faced his first class. He describes it as being 'held hand and foot by the superintendent and compelled to go on'. However, he settled quickly into his new responsibility. His early efforts taught him many very important lessons. 'When I began to teach — I was very young in grace then — I said to the class of boys whom I was teaching that Jesus Christ saved all those who believed in him. One of them at once asked the question, "Teacher, do you believe in him?" I replied, "Yes, I hope I do." Then he enquired again, "But are you not sure?" I had to think carefully what answer I should give. The lad was not content with my repeating, "I hope so." He would have it, "If you have believed in Christ, you are saved." And I felt at that time I could not teach effectually until I could say positively, "I know that it is so. I must be able to speak of what I have heard, and seen, and tasted, and handled of the good Lord of life." The boy was right; there can be no true testimony except that which springs from assured conviction of our own safety and joy in the Lord.'

It was the custom in the Newmarket Sunday School for one of the male teachers to speak to the whole school at the end of classes. The superintendent took it every other week and the other men in their turn. Charles' turn came and afterwards the superintendent asked him to take his place the following Sunday. Charles did so well that he was asked to speak every Sunday. He protested that this would not be fair on the other teachers, but his protests were overruled. This Sunday afternoon ministry was so blessed that many of the older people began to attend.

Spurgeon always had a high regard for Sunday School work. He complained that older, more experienced believers did not take enough interest in this important work, and left the teaching to young people. He said, 'He who teaches in a class in Sunday School has earned a good degree. I had rather receive the title S.S.T. (Sunday School teacher) than M.A., B.A. or any other honour that ever was conferred by men.'

Spiritual growth

In August 1850, his work as a school tutor took him to Cambridge and there he joined the Baptist Church. By this time his spiritual growth was very evident as can be seen from a letter he wrote to his father on 19 September.

My dear father,
   I received your kind letter in due time. I joined the church here at the Lord's table last ordinance day. I shall write for my dismission; I intended to have done so before. The Baptists are by far the most respectable denomination in Cambridge; there are three Baptist Chapels — St Andrew's Street, where we attend, Zion Chapel and Eden Chapel. There is a very fine Wesleyan Chapel and some others. I teach in the Sunday School all the afternoon. Mr Leeding takes the morning work. Last

Sabbath day we had a funeral sermon from Hebrews 6:11-12. We have a prayer meeting at 7 in the morning, and one after the evening service; they are precious means of grace, I trust, to my soul. How soon would the lamps go out did not our mighty Lord supply fresh oil; and if it were not for his unshaken promise to supply our need out of the fulness of his grace, poor indeed should we be.

Yes, when Jesus comes, he comes to reign: how I wish he would reign more in my heart! Then I might hope that every atom of self-confidence and self-righteousness would be quite swept out of my soul. I am sure I long for the time when all evil affections, corrupt desires, rebellions and doubting thoughts shall be overcome, and completely crushed beneath the Prince's feet, and my whole soul be made pure and holy. But so long as I am engaged within this house of clay, I know they will lurk about, and I must have hard fighting though the victory by grace is sure. Praying is the best fighting; nothing else will keep them down.

I have written a letter to grandfather; I am sorry he is poorly. He wants the promise now, and why may not young and old live upon them? They are the bread-corn of heaven, the meat of the kingdom, and who that has tasted them will turn to eat husks without any sweetness or comfort in them? God's power will keep all his children, while he says to them, "How shall we who are dead to sin live any longer therein?" I feel persuaded that I shall never fathom the depths of my own natural depravity, nor climb to the tops of the mountain of God's eternal love. I feel constrained day by day to fall flat down upon the promises, and leave my soul in Jesu's keeping. It is he that makes my feet move even in the slow obedience which marks them at present, and every attainment of grace must come from him. I would go forth by prayer, like the Israelites, to gather up this heavenly manna, and live upon free grace.

'Add to all your great kindness and love to me, through my life, a constant remembrance of me in your prayers. I thank you for those petitions which you and dear mother have so often sent up to the mercy seat for me. Give my love to my sisters and brother, and accept the same for yourself and dear mother. Hoping you are all quite well,

'I remain

'Your obedient, affectionate son,

Charles H. Spurgeon'

His first sermon

At Cambridge God began to prepare his young servant more deeply for the great work he had for him. In the St Andrew's Street Chapel there was a Preachers' Association. This brought together all the lay preachers in the church who took services in the villages around Cambridge. In charge of this was a remarkable character by the name of James Vinter. He was held in great esteem by the lay preachers and they referred to him, affectionately, as 'Bishop Vinter'. Spurgeon had the suspicion that the 'bishop' was not only an organizer and preacher, but also a recruiting sergeant. As events turned out this suspicion was fully justified.

One Saturday, James Vinter asked Charles if on the Sunday evening he would to to Teversham. There was a young man who was to preach who was not used to taking services, and he would be glad if someone went with him. The following day, after tea, Charles met another young man who was a couple of years older than himself, and they set out to walk to the chapel. They talked as they walked along, and Charles expressed the hope that his friend would know the presence of the Lord while preaching that evening. To his amazement, his companion assured him that he had never preached in his life and had no intention of preaching that evening. Charles protested that he was in the same position, and even if he was a preacher he had not prepared a sermon. The older boy replied more emphatically than ever that he could not preach and if Spurgeon did not preach there would be no sermon at all. He urged Charles to repeat one of his Sunday School talks, as that would probably be more suitable for simple country folks than a studied sermon.

There was no alternative. Young Spurgeon would have to preach his first sermon. This was, of course, exactly what James Vinter had planned. He knew Charles would never have agreed to preach, but this experienced recruiting sergeant was not put off by that. For the remainder of the journey there was little talk as Charles lifted his heart to God for help. He was very anxious but felt that at least he could tell the people of the love of Jesus and the story of the cross. His text would be, 'Unto you therefore which believe he is precious.' He prayed earnestly for God's blessing and no doubt 'Bishop' Vinter was also praying the same prayer.

The Lord answered those prayers, as Charles himself recounts for us: 'We entered the low-pitched room of the thatched cottage, where a few simple-minded farm-labourers and their wives were gathered together; we sang and prayed and read the Scriptures, and then came my first sermon. How long, or how short it was, I cannot remember. It was not half such a task as I had feared it would be, but I was glad to see my way to a fair conclusion, and to the giving out of the last hymn. To my delight, I had not broken down or stopped in the middle, nor been destitute of ideas, and the desired haven was in view. I made a finish, and took up the hymn book, but to my astonishment, an aged voice cried out, "Bless your dear heart, how old are you?" My very solemn reply was, "You must wait till the service is over before making such enquiries. Let us now sing." We did sing, the young preacher pronounced the benediction and then there began a dialogue which enlarged into a warm, friendly talk in which everybody appeared to take

The cottage at Teversham where Spurgeon preached his first sermon

part. "How old are you?" was the leading question. "I am under sixty," was the reply. "Yes, and under sixteen," was the old lady's rejoinder. "Never mind my age, think of the Lord Jesus and his preciousness," was all I could say, after promising that I would come again, if the gentlemen at Cambridge thought me fit to do so. Very great and profound was my awe of "the gentlemen at Cambridge" in those days.'

Preaching regularly

James Vinter's method of starting a preacher would not be one to recommend, but it was undoubtedly successful and began the ministry of one of the greatest preachers England has ever heard. From the first Sunday at Teversham, Charles began to preach regularly. Preaching to him was a very serious business that demanded a great deal of prayer and the reading of Scripture. His method of preparation in the early days was simple. He would soak himself in the Word of God, then on his walk to the service he would think over again what he had read. His preaching was to tell out simply and earnestly what he had first received into his own mind and heart.

He preached in the villages around Cambridge, sometimes in a chapel, but often in a farmer's kitchen, in a cottage or in a barn. He would walk three, five or even eight miles there and back, to minister the gospel. When it was wet, waterproof leggings, a mackintosh coat and a waterproof hat came into service, and on dark nights Charles carried a lantern. Like every young preacher, his first sermons contained many odd statements, but it was a happy training-school, used by God to develop Spurgeon's gift of preaching.

Preaching is more than just speaking out words to men and women, even though the words be the truths of the gospel. The preacher must have a heart that is sympathetic to the needs of people. That this heart was being moulded by God in Charles Spurgeon during this time is illustrated in one incident which he recounts.

'I had many adventures, and a great variety of experiences in this itinerant work. I recollect one summer's evening, when I had engaged to preach at a village not far from Waterbeach. Before I could reach my destination, the sky darkened, and a severe thunderstorm burst over the district. Some people are terrified at lightning, but ever since I believed in the Lord Jesus Christ, I have had no fear in a storm, however severe it might be.

'On this particular occasion, while walking to the place where I was to preach, I was enjoying the storm, but as I was passing a cottage on the road, I noticed a woman who seemed to be greatly alarmed and in sore distress because of the storm. I did not like to pass by, and leave a fellow creature in trouble, so I entered the house, read a few verses of Scripture, and prayed, and so comforted the woman. I then proceeded to my destination, to fulfil my engagement. On entering the village, I took off my waterproof coat, because the smooth surface seemed to reflect the vivid flashes of lightning in a way that might alarm the timid. I found that, because of the severity of the weather, the people were not expecting that there would be a service, so I went round from house to house, and invited them to come to the regular meeting-place. This unusual method of gathering a congregation brought me many hearers; the service was held, and, at its close, I walked back to my Cambridge home.'

Hearing other preachers

A man who loves to preach, as young Spurgeon so obviously did, will inevitably be a man who loves to hear preaching. Two preachers that were a particular blessing to him as a teenager were William Jay of Bath and John Angell James of Birmingham.

Jay was an old man when Spurgeon heard him preach on the text, 'Let your conversation be as it becometh the gospel of Christ.' He never forgot the dignity and simplicity with which William Jay preached. One remark that deeply impressed his

young mind was, 'You do need a mediator between yourselves and God, but you do not need a mediator between
yourselves and Christ; you may come to him just as you are.'

John Angell James was one of the most famous preachers
of his time. Birmingham was not easy to get to, but Charles
was so anxious to hear James that he saved money from his
very small income to make the journey. Spurgeon says of that
sermon, 'I heard him deliver a week-evening lecture, in the
large vestry, on the precious text, "Ye are complete in him."
The savour of that very sweet discourse abides with me to this
day, and I shall never read the passage without associating it
with the quiet but earnest utterances of that eminent man of
God. Years afterwards, on being in James' company, I told
him that I went all the way from Cambridge to Birmingham to
hear him preach. On my mentioning the text, he replied, "Ah!
that was a Calvinistic sermon. You would enjoy that, but you
would not get on with me always." I was glad also to have the
opportunity of thanking him for that precious book of his, *The
Anxious Enquirer*, which has been the means of bringing so
many sinners to the Saviour, and which I found exceedingly
helpful when I was seeking the Lord.'

A sermon outline

It would be easy to forget that Spurgeon at this time was still
only sixteen years old. What content would there be to a
sermon preached by such a young person? We are fortunate
that we can answer that question accurately by looking at the
outline of one of his sermons preached in 1851.

'Having predestinated us unto the adoption of children by
Jesus Christ to himself, according to the good pleasure of his
will' (Ephesians 1:5).

Meaning of the term.
Common among Romans.

Two instances in Scripture, Moses and Esther.
Adoption differs from justification and regeneration.

I The sense in which believers are sons of God
Not as Jesus. More so than creatures.
1. In some things spiritual adoption agrees with civil
1. In name and thing.
2. To an inheritance.
3. Voluntary on the part of the adopter.
4. Taking the adopter's name.
5. Received into the family.
6. Considered as children: food, protection, clothing, education, attendance provided.
7. Under the control of the father.
2. In some things they disagree
1. Civil adoption requires the consent of the adopted.
2. Civil adoption was intended to provide for childless persons.
3. In civil adoption, the adopted had something to recommend him.
4. The nature of a son could not be given.
5. The children did not inherit till their father's death.
6. The pontifex might make it void.

II The cause of adoption
1. The persons: God; Father, Son, Spirit.
2. The motive: free grace, not works.

III The objects of it
Elect sinners, not angels.
All believers.
Not all men, but justified men.

IV The excellency of it
1. It is an act of surprising grace (1 John 3:1). Consider the persons.
2. It exceeds all others.

3. It makes men honourable.
4. Brings men into the highest relations.
5. Includes all things.
6. Immutable and everlasting.

V The effects of it
1. Share in the love, pity and care of God.
2. Access with boldness.
3. Conformity to the image of Jesus.
4. The Holy Spirit.
5. Heirship.
Encouragement. Appeal to saints and sinners.

8.
Waterbeach

In 1851, at the age of seventeen, Spurgeon became the pastor of a small Baptist church of forty members in the village of Waterbeach. Initially the church could not financially support him and he continued to work in the school at Cambridge. Part-time pastoring was not to the liking of this teenager and after a while he resigned his position in Cambridge and became full time at Waterbeach. The church could still not pay him a living wage but this did not deter him. 'They gave me a salary of £45 a year, but as I had to pay 12s [60p] a week for two rooms which I occupied, my income was not sufficient to support me, but the people, though they had not money, had produce, and I do not think there was a pig killed by any one of the congregation without my having some portion of it, and one or other of them, when coming to market at Cambridge, would bring me bread and meat to pay rent with, and I often paid my landlady in that fashion.'

Deacons

Being the pastor of a church at seventeen is an almost imposs-ible task, and even for an exceptionally gifted youngster like Spurgeon it could easily have proved too much. But God, in his goodness, supplied Charles with an excellent body of deacons

Waterbeach, the scene of
Spurgeon's first pastorate

to support him. They were men totally committed to the Lord's work and there developed a relationship between the pastor and the deacons of respect and sincere love.

These men were able to guide the teenage pastor and when necessary issue a needed rebuke. This was especially true of one of the deacons, a man by the name of King. 'He was a methodical man, and kept the accounts and the church books in an admirable order. He was a calm, thoughtful, judicious brother but he had a full proportion of zeal and warmth. His wife was made to match, and the pair were second to none in the village for grace and wisdom. Mr King once gave me a kindly hint in a very delicate manner. He did not tell me that I should speak more guardedly in the pulpit, but when I left his house, one Monday morning, I found a pin in my Bible, stuck through Titus 2:8: "Sound speech, that cannot be condemned; that he that is of the contrary part may be ashamed, having no evil thing to say of you." Nothing could have been in better taste. The wise rebuke was well deserved and lovingly taken. It was so deftly given that its value was thereby increased immeasurably. Mr King was a deacon of deacons to me, and to the Waterbeach Church.'

Charles did not always heed the advice of his deacons. On one occasion he proposed that they hold an open-air service by the riverside on Sunday evenings. One of the deacons was not in favour because open-air preaching would be 'imitating the Methodists'. The pastor was not put off by such an objection. All through his ministry he believed passionately in the need to take the gospel to the people. 'All over England, in our cities, towns, villages, hamlets, there are tens of thousands who never hear the gospel while open-air preaching is neglected. I rejoice that God allows us to preach in churches and chapels, but I do not pretend that we have apostolic precedent for it, certainly none for confining our ministry to such places. I believe that we are permitted, if it promotes order and edification, to set apart buildings for our worship, but there is no warrant for calling these places sanctuaries and houses of God, for all places are alike holy where holy men assemble. It is a mischievous thing that we should confine preaching within walls. Our Lord, it is true, preached in the synagogues, but he often spoke on the mountain-side, or from a boat, or in the court-house, or in the public thoroughfares. To him, an audience was the only necessity. He was a fisher of souls of the true sort, and not like those who sit still in their houses, and expect the fish to come to them to be caught. Did our Lord intend a minister to go on preaching from his pulpit to empty pews, when, by standing on a chair or a table outside the meeting-house, he might be heard by hundreds? I believe not, and I held the same opinion at the very beginning of my ministry, so I preached by the riverside, even though my good deacon thought that, by doing so, I was imitating the Methodists.'

The first convert

Spurgeon was a faithful preacher of the gospel of God's grace, but he was never satisfied with merely being faithful. He longed to see souls saved through his preaching. He would anxiously ask his deacons, 'Have you heard of anyone finding the Lord under my ministry?' They would try to encourage him by saying, 'I am sure somebody must have received the Saviour.' This to him was not good enough. 'But I want to know it,' he said, 'I want to prove that it is so.'

Waterbeach was not an easy place in which to minister. It was an extremely poor village, notorious for its drunkenness and profanity. To such a place God sent a seventeen-year-old preacher with a heart burning for the divine glory and the salvation of the lost. The news of the first convert brought an overwhelming sense of joy to Spurgeon's young heart. One Sunday afternoon, a deacon said to him, 'God has set his seal on your ministry in this place.' Apparently a few Sundays previously a poor labourer's wife had gone home from the services under deep conviction of sin. Eventually she had found peace with God and was now asking to speak with the pastor. Charles saw her the next day. Of that woman he said, 'I have in my eye now the cottage in which she lived; believe me, it always appears picturesque. I felt like the boy who had earned his first guinea, or like a diver who has been down to the depths of the sea, and brought up a rare pearl. I prize each one whom God has given me, but I prize that woman most. Since then, my Lord has blessed me to many thousands of souls, who have found the Saviour by hearing or reading the words which have come from my lips. I have had a great many spiritual children born of the preaching of the Word, but I still think that woman was the best of the lot. At least, she did not live long enough for me to find faults in her. After a year or two of faithful witness-bearing, she went home, to lead the way for a godly number who have followed her. I remember well her being received into the church, and dying, and going to heaven. She was the first seal to my ministry, and a very precious one.'

Disappointment

All professions of faith did not bring the same joy. One man in particular caused the young pastor great sorrow. This man was a big fellow who was notorious as a drunkard and a thoroughly evil man. It therefore caused a sensation in the village when he went to hear Spurgeon preach. He professed conversion and showed every sign outwardly of being a changed character. He gave up his swearing and drinking, began attending the chapel regularly and even prayed in the prayer meeting. The village was astonished, and Spurgeon regarded him as 'a bright jewel in the Redeemer's crown'.

For nine months everything went well; then the problems began. 'The laughter to which he was exposed, the jeers and scoffs of his old companions — though at first he bore them like a man — became too much for him. He began to think that he had been a little too fanatical, a little too earnest. He slunk up to the place of worship instead of coming in boldly; he gradually forsook the weeknight service, and he neglected the Sabbath day; and, though warned and often rebuked, he returned to his old habits, and any thoughts of God or godliness that he had ever known seemed to die away. He could again utter the blasphemers' oath, once more he could act wickedly with the profane; and he — of whom we had often boasted, and said in our prayer meetings, "Oh, how much is God glorified by this man's conversion! What cannot divine grace do?" — to the confusion of us all, was to be seen sometimes drunk in our streets, and it was thrown in our teeth, "This is one of your Christians, is it? — one of your converts gone back again, and become as bad as he was before?"'

Unfortunately most pastors face such disappointments at some time in their ministries. To a young man like Spurgeon it could have been devastating. However, he was wise enough to see that the man had been more attracted to the preacher than to the Saviour. Such 'conversions' will always go the same way. Fortunately, to encourage the young man, there were many true conversions. The lives of many drunkards and criminals were completely changed not for a few months, but for ever. In the short period of just over two years that he ministered in Waterbeach, the village was transformed. 'I can say, with joy and happiness, that almost from one end of the village to the other, at the hour of eventide, one might have heard the voice of song coming from nearly every rooftop, and echoing from almost every heart. I do testify to the praise of God's grace, that it pleased the Lord to work wonders in our midst. He showed the power of Jesu's name, and made me a witness of that gospel which can win souls, draw reluctant hearts, and mould afresh the life and conduct of sinful men and women.'

College

Soon after he began at Waterbeach, Charles was strongly advised by his friends to enter the Baptist College at Stepney to prepare more fully for the ministry. His father was also very keen on this. It is not difficult to appreciate the thinking behind this advice. Spurgeon was still only seventeen, and normally this was much too young to be a pastor. A college course would not only further his education but also broaden his experience. All this was good, sound common sense, but Charles had no desire at all to go to college. It was not because he was against training for the ministry, for in a few years he himself would be starting a Pastors' College to prepare young men for the work of God. The simple reason was that he felt no leading of God towards the college.

When the idea was first mentioned he felt favourably inclined towards it. Dr Angus, a tutor of the college, was visiting Cambridge and it was arranged for young Spurgeon to meet him. He arrived at the meeting place at the appointed time and was shown by a maid into the drawing room. Dr Angus was waiting in the parlour but the maid forgot to tell him that Charles had arrived. The tutor and the prospective student sat waiting for each other in different rooms in the same house for a couple of hours, and they never met. The maid's mistake Spurgeon interpreted as the providence of God.

Soon afterwards Charles was walking alone in the country-side when he distinctly heard a loud voice say to him, 'Seekest thou great things for thyself? Seek them not!' He said of this experience, 'This led me to look at my position from another point of view, and to challenge my motives and intentions. I remembered the poor but loving people to whom I ministered, and the souls which had been given me in my humble charge; and, although at the time I anticipated obscurity and poverty as the result of the resolve, yet I did there and then solemnly renounce the offer of collegiate instruction, determining to abide for a season at least with my people, and to remain preaching the Word so long as I had strength to do it.'

In a letter to his father, dated 24 February 1852, he listed four reasons why he believed it would be wrong to go to college at that time:

1. Whatever advantages are to be derived from such a course of study, I shall be more able to improve when my powers are more developed than they are at present. When I know more, I shall be more able to learn.

2. Providence has thrown me into a great sphere of usefulness — a congregation of often 450, a loving church and an awakened audience. Many already own that the preaching has been with power from heaven. Now, ought I to leave them?

3. In a few years' time, I hope to improve my financial position, so as to be of no expense to you, or at least not for all. I should not like to know that you were burdening yourself for me. I should love to work my own way as much as possible. I know you like this feeling.

4. I am not uneducated. I have many opportunities of improvement now; all I want is more time; but even that, Mr Leeding would give me, if it were so arranged. I have plenty of practice, and do we not learn to preach by preaching? You know what my style is. I fancy it is not very college-like. Let it be never so bad, God has blessed it, and I believe he will yet more. All I do right, he does in me, and the might is of him. I am now well off; I think as well off as anyone of my age, and I am quite happy. If I were in need, I think the people might be able to raise more for me. Now, shall I throw myself out, and trust to Providence as to whether I shall ever get another place as soon as I leave college?

By this time, the friends at Cambridge who had first urged him to go to college were having second thoughts. The reason for this was the remarkable blessing upon the ministry at Waterbeach. It appears that the only one who was keen for Charles to go to Stepney was his father. This prompted Mr King, one of the Waterbeach deacons, to write to John Spurgeon on 20 March.

Dear Sir,

Having heard, with deep regret, of your intention of placing your son at Stepney College, I write to say that, if you were aware of all the circumstances connected with his ministry at Waterbeach, I think you would defer doing so, at least for a time.

Allow me to say that, since his coming, the congregation is very much increased, the aisles and vestry being often full, and many go away for want of room; there are several cases of his being made useful in awakening the careless; and although we have only known him about five months, the attachment is as strong as if we had been acquainted with him as many years, and if he were to leave us just now, it would be the occasion of general 'lamentation, mourning, and woe'. Added to which, he has no wish to go, but rather the reverse; and his friends at Cambridge, who previously recommended his going, now hesitate, and feel disposed to alter their opinion. If you, sir, could come over, and see for yourself, you would find that this account is not exaggerated, but perhaps would be ready to exclaim, 'The half was not told me.' That we may be divinely directed to act as shall be most conducive to the promotion of the Redeemer's glory, in connection with the best interests of those around us, is the sincere and earnest prayer of

Yours respectfully

C. King

on behalf of the church and congregation.

P.S. Our friends are very anxious that Mr Spurgeon should continue with us for at least a year. Your acceding to this would cause devout thanksgiving to God, and we hope would be attended with lasting benefit to many amongst us. A line to this effect would much oblige.

The matter was settled and Charles wrote to his mother in November 1852: 'I am more and more glad that I never went to college. God sends such sunshine on my path, such smiles of grace, that I cannot regret if I have forfeited all my prospects for it. I am conscious that I held back from love to God and his cause, and I had rather be poor in his service than rich in my own. I have all the heart can wish for; yea, God giveth more than my desire. My congregation is as great and loving as ever. During all the time that I have been at Waterbeach, I have had a different house for my home every Sabbath day. Fifty-two families have thus taken me in, and I have still other invitations not yet accepted. Talk about the people not caring for me, because they give me so little! I dare tell anybody under heaven, tis false! They do all they can. Our anniversary passed off grandly: six were baptized; crowds on crowds stood by the river; the chapel afterwards crammed, both to the tea and the sermon.'

9.
The Calvinist

Spurgeon never did have any formal theological training, but he was none the poorer for this. It was quite normal for him to live and think in the realm of theological truths and doctrines. He was always a humorous man, but never a frivolous one, and early in his life, his heart and mind embraced the great biblical truths that history has called Calvinism.

He said, 'It is a great thing to begin the Christian life by believing good solid doctrine. Some people have received twenty different "gospels" in as many years; how many more they will accept before they get to their journey's end, it would be difficult to predict. I thank God that he early taught me the gospel, and I have been so perfectly satisfied with it that I do not want to know any other. Constant change of creed is sure loss. If a tree is to be taken up two or three times a year, you will not need to build a very large loft in which to store the apples. When people are always shifting their doctrinal principles, they are not likely to bring forth much fruit to the glory of God. It is good for young believers to begin with a firm hold upon those great fundamental doctrines which the Lord has taught in his Word. Why, if I believed what some preach about the temporary, trumpery salvation which only lasts for a time I would scarcely be at all grateful for it; but when I know that those whom God saves he saves with an everlasting salvation, when I know that he gives them an everlasting right-eousness, when I know that he settles them on an everlasting foundation of everlasting love, and that he will bring them to his everlasting kingdom, oh, then I wonder, and I am astonished that such a blessing as this should ever have been given to me!'

Calvinism to him was only another way of describing the biblical theology of the Lord Jesus Christ and the apostle Paul. He said, 'We use the term then, not because we impute any extraordinary importance to Calvin's having taught these doctrines. We should be just as willing to call them by any other name, if we could find one which would be better understood, and which on the whole would be as consistent with fact.

'If anyone should ask me what I mean by a Calvinist, I should reply, "He is one who says, 'Salvation is of the Lord.'" I cannot find in Scripture any other doctrine than this. It is the essence of the Bible. "He only is my rock and my salvation." Tell me anything contrary to this truth, and it will be a heresy. Tell me a heresy, and I shall find its essence here, that it has departed from this great fundamental, this rock truth, "God is my rock and my salvation." What is the heresy of Rome, but the addition of something to the perfect merits of Jesus Christ — the bringing of the works of the flesh to assist in our justification? And what is the heresy of Arminianism but the addition of something to the work of the Redeemer? Every heresy, if brought to the touch-stone, will discover itself here. I have my own private opinion that there is no such thing as preaching Christ and him crucified, unless we preach what nowadays is called Calvinism. It is a nickname to call it Calvinism; Calvinism is the gospel and nothing else. I do not believe we can preach the gospel if we do not preach justification by faith, without works, nor unless we preach the sovereignty of God in his dispensation of grace; nor unless we exalt the electing, unchangeable, eternal, immutable, conquering love of Jehovah; nor do I think we can preach the gospel, unless we base it upon the special and particular redemption of his elect and chosen people which Christ wrought out upon the cross, nor can I comprehend a gospel which lets saints fall away after they have been called, and suffers the children of God to be burned in the fires of damnation after having once believed in Jesus. Such a gospel I abhor!'

The whole of Spurgeon's preaching obviously flowed out of this doctrine. The sovereignty of God was the key to everything, and truths like election, perseverance and particular redemption were not to be apologized for but proclaimed with passion and authority. The following paragraphs show in his own words what he believed concerning these great doctrines.

Election

'John Newton used to tell a whimsical story, and laugh at it, too, of a good woman who said, in order to prove the doctrine of election, "Ah, sir, the Lord must have loved me before I was born, or else he would not have seen anything in me to love afterwards!" I am sure it is true in my case; I believe the doctrine of election because I am quite certain that if God had not chosen me, I should never have chosen him; and I am sure he chose me before I was born, or else he never would have chosen me afterwards; and he must have elected me for reasons unknown to me, for I never could find any reason in myself why he should have looked upon me with special love. So I am forced to accept that great biblical doctrine.'

'In the very beginning, when this great universe lay in the mind of God, like unborn forests in the acorn cup; long ere the lights flashed through the sky, God loved his chosen creatures. Before there was any created being, their names were written on his heart, and then were they dear to his soul. Jesus loved his people before the foundation of the world — even from eternity! And when he called me by his grace, he said to me, "I have loved thee with an everlasting love: therefore with loving-kindness have I drawn thee."'

Final perseverance

'If one dear saint of God had perished, so might all; if one of the covenant ones be lost, so may all be; and then there is no gospel promise true, but the Bible is a lie, and there is nothing in it worth my acceptance. I will be an infidel at once when I can believe that a saint of God can ever fall finally. If God hath loved me once, then he will love me for ever.'

'I do not know how some people, who believe that a Christian can fall from grace, manage to be happy. It must be a very commendable thing in them to be able to get through a day without despair. If I did not believe the doctrine of the final perseverance of the saints, I think I should be of all men most miserable, because I should lack any ground of comfort.'

Particular redemption

'Some persons love the doctrine of universal atonement because they say, "It is so beautiful. It is a lovely idea that Christ should have died for all men; it commends itself," they say, "to the instincts of humanity; there is something in it full of joy and beauty." I admit there is, but beauty may be often associated with falsehood. There is much which I admire in the theory of universal redemption, but I will just show what the supposition necessarily involved. If Christ on his cross intended to save every man, then he intended to save those who were lost before he died. If the doctrine be true that he died for all men, then he died for some who were in hell before he came into this world; for doubtless there were even then myriads there who had been cast away because of their sins. Once again, if it was Christ's intention to save all men, how deplorably has he been disappointed, for we have his own testimony that there is a lake which burneth with fire and brimstone, and into that pit of woe have been cast some of the very persons who, according to the theory of universal redemption, were bought with his blood. That seems to me a conception a thousand times more repulsive than any of those consequences which are said to be associated with the Calvinistic and Christian doctrine of special and particular redemption. To think that my Saviour died for men who were or are in hell seems a supposition too horrible for me to entertain. To imagine for a moment that he was the substitute for all the sons of men, and that God, having first punished the substitute, afterwards punished the sinners themselves, seems to conflict with all my ideas of divine justice. That Christ should offer an atonement and satisfaction for the sins of all men, and that afterwards some of those very men should be punished for the sins for which Christ atoned, appears to me to be the most monstrous iniquity that could ever have been imputed to Saturn, to Janus, to the goddess of the Thugs, or to the most diabolical heathen deities. God forbid that we should ever think thus of Jehovah, the just and wise and good!'

Controversy

Spurgeon's doctrine was not cold, arid, intellectualism but warm, passionate and evangelistic. He loved the Lord Jesus Christ, and delighted to make a 'bee-line' for the Saviour in every sermon. He longed to see souls saved and his preaching was directed to that end. Thus his Calvinism was what all true Bible-centred Calvinism ought to be. It was the Calvinism that had fired the great revivals of previous centuries, and that had inspired the great missionary movement to take the gospel to the far corners of the world. But it was not the doctrinal position that was popular in England in Spurgeon's day. Evangelicalism in the mid-nineteenth century, as it is today, was in the main doctrinally Arminian and not Calvinistic.

The difference between the two systems of theology has been summarized by Dr J. I. Packer: 'The difference between them is not primarily one of emphasis but of content. One proclaims a God who saves; the other speaks of a God who enables man to save himself. One view presents the three great acts of the Holy Trinity for the recovering of lost mankind — election by the Father, redemption by the Son, calling by the Spirit — as directed towards the same persons, and as securing their salvation infallibly. The other view gives each act a different reference (the objects of redemption being all mankind, of calling, those who hear the gospel, and of election, those hearers who respond), and denies that any man's salvation is secured by any of them. The two theologies thus conceive the plan of salvation in quite different terms. One makes salvation depend on the work of God, the other on the work of man; one regards faith as part of God's gift of salvation, the other as man's contribution to salvation; one gives all the glory of saving believers to God, the other divides the praise between God, who, so to speak, built the machinery of salvation, and man, who, by believing, operated it.'

Spurgeon's doctrine was not popular among his fellow-evangelicals, and he himself became unpopular because of his open and vigorous opposition to Arminianism.

He said in a sermon preached on 28 February 1858, 'The Arminian holds that Christ, when he died, did not die with an intent to save any particular person: and he teaches that Christ's death does not in itself secure, beyond doubt, the salvation of any one man living ... they are obliged to hold that if man's will would not give way, and voluntarily surrender to grace, then Christ's atonement would be unavailing ... We say Christ so died that he infallibly secured the salvation of a multitude that no man can number, who through Christ's death not only may be saved, but are saved, must be saved, and cannot by any possibility run the hazard of being anything but saved.'

Two years later, on 3 June 1860, he said, 'What the Arminian wants to do is to arouse man's activity; what we want to do is to kill it once and for all, to show him that he is lost and ruined, and that his activities are not at all equal to the work of conversion — that he must look upward. They seek to make the man stand up; we seek to bring him down, and make him feel that there he lies in the hand of God, and must cry aloud, "Lord, save, or we perish."

'We hold that man is never so near grace as when he begins to feel he can do nothing at all. When he says, "I can pray, I can believe, I can do this, and I can do the other," marks of self-sufficiency and arrogance are on his brow.'

This was typical of his preaching, not only as a young man, but throughout his life. It was not that he was argumentative and self-opinionated, but he believed passionately that Arminian doctrine was distorting the gospel. Spurgeon was not a small-minded man, and his convictions in the Calvinism-Arminianism controversy never degenerated into a 'party spirit'. While differing strongly with fellow-believers on doctrine he was still able to love them and to speak warmly of their Christian devotion. He once said, 'There is no soul living who holds more firmly to the doctrines of grace than I do, and if any man asks me whether I am ashamed to be called a Calvinist, I answer, I wished to be called nothing but a Christian; but if you ask me, do I hold the doctrinal views which were held by John Calvin, I reply, I do in the main hold them, and rejoice to avow it. But far be it from me to imagine that Zion contains none but Calvinistic Christians within her walls, or that there are none saved who do not hold our views. Most atrocious things have been spoken about the character and spiritual condition of John Wesley, the modern prince of Arminians. I can only say concerning him that, while I detest many of the doctrines which he preached, yet for the man himself I have a reverence second to no Wesleyan; and if there wanted two apostles to be added to the number of the twelve, I do not believe that there could be found two men more fit to be added than George Whitefield and John Wesley. The character of John Wesley stands beyond all imputation of self-sacrifice, zeal, holiness and communion with God; he lived far above the ordinary level of common Christians, and was one "of whom the word was not worthy". I believe there are multitudes of men who cannot see these truths, or, at least, cannot see them in the way which we put them, who nevertheless have received Christ as their Saviour, and are as dear to the heart of the God of grace as the soundest Calvinist in or out of heaven.'

Unfortunately the same charity was not always extended to him. When he came to London in 1854, as a young man of nineteen, to take up the pastorate at New Park Street Chapel, he received little help or guidance from his fellow-ministers. In 1856 he said, 'Scarcely a minister looks on us or speaks favourably of us, because we hold strong views upon the divine sovereignty of God, and his divine electings and special love towards his own people.' This opposition did not ease off, and addressing his congregation in 1860, he said, 'There has been no single church of God existing in England for these fifty years which has had to pass through more trial than we have done ... scarce a day rolls over my head in which the most villainous abuse, the most fearful slander is not uttered against me both privately and by the public press. Every engine is employed to put down God's minister — every lie that man can invent is hurled at me... They have not checked our usefulness as a church; they have not thinned our congregations; that which was to be but a spasm — an enthusiasm which it was hoped would last an hour — God has daily increased; not because of me, but because of that gospel which I preach; not because there was anything in me, but because I came out as the exponent of plain, straight-forward, honest Calvinism, and because I seek to speak the Word simply.'

Spurgeon was a sensitive man and the bitterness of the opposition distressed him greatly, but it never diminished in the slightest what he believed and preached.

10.
New Park Street

When still only nineteen years old and pastoring at Waterbeach, Spurgeon received an invitation to preach at New Park Street Chapel in London. It came as a great surprise to him, but he accepted the invitation and preached on 11 December 1853. The church at New Park Street was greatly attracted to the young preacher and he further agreed to minister to them on 1, 15 and 29 January. Before the third of those engagements was fulfilled, on 25 January the church invited Spurgeon to occupy their pulpit for a trial period of six months. He accepted and with great reluctance left his flock at Waterbeach.

God's blessing was mighty upon his preaching and the six months' trial was never concluded. On 19 April 1854, the church at New Park Street called the young Spurgeon to be its permanent pastor. On 28 April he accepted, and thus began one of the most remarkable pastorates in the history of the Christian church.

The congregation at New Park Street was in decline when Spurgeon went there. It was, in his own words, 'a mere handful of people'. Actually, there were 200 who worshipped there regularly. By today's standards that would be a strong church, but in 1854 it was a mere handful. Obviously, to the new pastor it was a small church, but he was in no doubt that these believers had a great spiritual strength. They were a praying

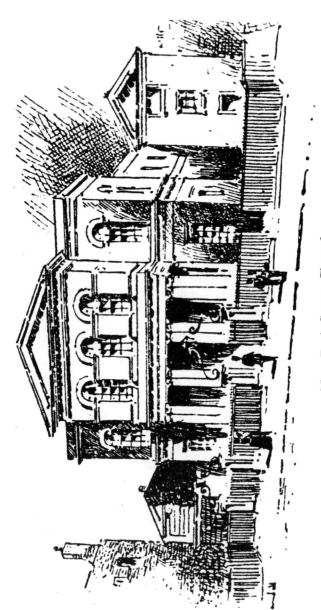

New Park Street Chapel

people. They knew how to plead with God. 'We had prayer meetings in New Park Street that moved our very souls. Every man seemed like a crusader besieging the New Jerusalem, each one appeared determined to storm the Celestial City by the might of intercession, and soon the blessing came upon us in such abundance that we had not room to receive it.'

The combination of the preaching gifts of Spurgeon and the prayers of the church was mighty in the hand of God. The congregation multiplied rapidly and soon the twelve hundred seats were all full Sunday after Sunday.

The spiritual blessing created physical problems. A packed building, with gas lights burning, was not the most comfortable place, particularly as the windows were not made to open. Charles urged the deacons to do something about the lack of air. On several occasions he asked them to remove the upper panes of glass, but nothing was done. In the end he solved the problem himself with the aid of his walking stick! The chapel building was only just over twenty years old and the deacons seemed reluctant to do any structural alterations to accommodate the growing congregation. In sheer frustration Spurgeon was moved one night in the middle of a sermon to declare, 'By faith the walls of Jericho fell down, and by faith, this wall at the back shall come down too.' After the service one of the older and more prudent deacons rebuked him with the words: 'Let us never hear of that again.' Spurgeon replied, 'You will hear no more about it when it is done, and therefore the sooner you set about it the better.'

The pastor had his way, and at a church meeting on 30 August 1854, the following resolution was passed: 'That we desire, as a church, to record our devout and grateful acknowledgements to our heavenly Father for the success that has attended the ministry of our esteemed pastor and we consider it important, at as early a period as possible, that increased accommodation should be provided for the numbers that flock to the chapel on the Lord's days; and we would affectionately request our respected deacons to give the subject their full and careful consideration, and to favour us with their report at the church meeting in October.'

Spurgeon with the deacons of New Park Street Chapel

Wisdom

Success is always a dangerous thing to handle. This is particularly true for a young man. Pride and arrogance can often follow rapidly on the heels of success with devastating effects. When such amazing success came to the nineteen-year-old Spurgeon he was spared the problems of pride. In fact his reaction was quite the opposite; his success frightened him: 'I hope I was not faithless, but I was timorous, and filled with a sense of my own unfitness. I dreaded the work which a gracious Providence had prepared for me. I felt myself a mere child, and trembled as I heard the voice which said, "Arise, and thresh the mountains, and make them as chaff."'

God's hand was obviously upon this young pastor. He was spared the awful spiritual paralysis of pride and given a wisdom that was far beyond his years. A new pastor inevitably has to face problems inherited from the previous ministry. Spurgeon was no exception, but his approach to the situation was perfect: 'I am quite certain that, for my own success, and for the prosperity of the church, I took the wisest course by applying my blind eye to all disputes which dated previously to my advent. It is the extremity of unwisdom for a young man, fresh from college, or from another charge, to suffer himself to be earwigged by a clique, and to be bribed by kindness and flattery to become a partisan, and so to ruin himself with one-half of his people.'

Wisdom is not only needed to handle the complaints of Christians but also to deal with the searchings of sinners.

'Once, when I was in the vestry, an Irishman came to see me. Pat began by making a low bow, and saying, "Now, your riverance, I have come to ax you a question."

'"Oh!" said I, "Pat, I am not a riverance; it is not a title I care for; but what is your question, and how is it you have not been to your priest about it?"

'He said, "I have been to him, but I don't like his answer."

'"Well, what is your question?"

'Said he, "God is just; and if God is just, he must punish my sins. I deserve to be punished. If he is a just God, he ought to punish me; yet you say God is merciful, and will forgive sins. I cannot see how that is right; he has no right to do that. He ought to be just, and punish those who deserve it. Tell me how God can be just and yet be merciful."

'I replied, "That is through the blood of Christ."

'"Yes," said he, "that is what my priest says. You are very much alike there; but he said a good deal besides, that I did not understand; and that short answer does not satisfy me. I want to know how it is that the blood of Jesus Christ enables God to be just, and yet to be merciful."

'Then I saw what he wanted to know, and explained the plan of salvation thus: "Now, Pat, suppose you had been killing a man, and the judge said, 'That Irishman must be hanged.'"

'He said quickly, "And I should have richly deserved to be hanged."

'"But, Pat, suppose I was fond of you, can you see any way by which I could save you from being hanged?"

'"No, sir, I cannot."

'"Then suppose I went to the queen and said, 'Please your Majesty, I am very fond of this Irishman; I think the judge was quite right in saying that he must be hanged, but let me be hanged instead, and you will then carry out the law.' Now, the queen could not agree to my proposal; but suppose she could — and God can, for he has power greater than all kings and queens — suppose the queen should have hanged me instead of you, do you think the policeman would take you up afterwards?"

'He at once said, "No, I should think not; they would not meddle with me; but if they did, I should say, 'What are you doing? Did not that gentleman condescend to be hung for me? Let me alone; shure, you don't want to hang two people for the same thing, do ye?'"

'I replied to the Irishman, "Ah, my friend, you have hit it; that is the way whereby we are saved! God must punish sin. Christ said, 'My Father, punish me instead of the sinner,' and his Father did. God laid on his beloved Son, Jesus Christ, the whole burden of our sins, and all their punishment and chastisement; and now that Christ is punished instead of us, God would not be just if he were to punish any sinner who believes on the Lord Jesus Christ. If thou believest in Jesus Christ, the well-beloved and only begotten Son of God, thou art saved, and thou mayest go on thy way rejoicing.

"'Faith," said the man, clapping his hands, "That's the gospel. Pat is safe now; with all his sins about him, he'll trust in the man that died fir him, and so he shall be saved."'

Cholera

1854 was the year of a terrible outbreak of cholera in London. The New Park Street congregation suffered like everyone else and their pastor was kept busy visiting family after family. At first Spurgeon threw himself vigorously into this desperate work, but gradually the sight of so much suffering and death was more than he could bear.

One day he was on his way home after a funeral feeling particularly depressed. Walking down Great Dover Road he saw, in the window of a shoemaker's shop, these words from Psalm 91: 'Because thou hast made the Lord, which is my refuge, even the Most High, thy habitation; there shall no evil befall thee, neither shall any plague come nigh thy dwelling.' He said, 'The effect upon my heart was immediate. Faith appropriated the passage as her own. I felt secure, refreshed, girt with immortality. I went on with my visitation of the dying, in a calm and peaceful spirit; I felt no fear of evil, and I suffered no harm. The providence which moved the tradesman to place those verses in his window I gratefully acknowledge, and in the remembrance of its marvellous power, I adore the Lord my God.'

During the epidemic Spurgeon saw many die who had no faith in Christ. One such man sent for him in his dying moments but the pastor was unable to give him any spiritual

The text in the window

help. Of that experience he said, 'That man, in his lifetime, had been wont to jeer at me. In strong language, he had often denounced me as a hypocrite. Yet he was no sooner smitten by the darts of death than he sought my presence and counsel, no doubt feeling in his heart that I was a servant of God, though he did not care to own it with his lips. There I stood, unable to help him. Promptly as I responded to his call, what could I do but look at his corpse, and mourn over a lost soul? He had, when in health, wickedly refused Christ, yet in his death-agony he had superstitiously sent for me. Too late he sighed for the ministry of reconciliation, and sought to enter in at the closed door, but he was not able. There was no space left for him then for repentance, for he had wasted the opportunities which God had long granted him. I went home, and was soon called away again; that time, to see a young woman. She also was in the last extremity, but it was a fair, fair sight. She was singing though she knew she was dying, and talking to those round about her, telling her brothers and sisters to follow her to heaven, bidding goodbye to her father, and all the while smiling as if it had been her marriage day. She was happy and blessed. I never saw more conspicuously in my life, than I did that morning, the difference there is between one who feareth God and one who feareth him not.'

Love

In the congregation at New Park Street was a young girl named Susannah Thompson. She had been converted about a year before the new pastor started his ministry, but was by then in a backslidden state. Spurgeon's preaching dealt with her so effectively that she earnestly sought spiritual help from one of the Sunday School staff. Soon the pastor was involved in helping her, and of his counsel she said, 'By degrees, though with much trembling, I told him of my state before God; and he gently led me, by his preaching and his conversation, through the power of the Holy Spirit, to the cross of Christ for the peace and pardon my weary soul was longing for.'

Susannah Spurgeon

Pastoral concern turned to deep love and by August 1854 everyone was aware of the new relationship that existed between Charles and Susannah. The following February Spurgeon baptized his fiancée, and they were married on 8 January 1856.

Opposition

The impact of Spurgeon's preaching upon London was amazing. By the beginning of 1855 the chapel in New Park Street was too small to accommodate the crowds attending and urgent work began on enlarging the building. In the meanwhile, the services were held in the Exeter Hall. Such success was not good news to everyone concerned with the religious life of London, and soon the young preacher was the target of a vicious series of articles and letters in the public press. The writers were mainly ministers and church people.

The Rev. Charles Banks wrote in the *Earthen Vessel* December 1854, 'Mr C. H. Spurgeon is the present pastor of New Park Street Chapel, in the borough of Southwark. He is a young man of a very considerable ministerial talent, and his labours have been amazingly successful in raising up the drooping cause at Park Street to a state of prosperity almost unequalled. We know of no Baptist minister in all the metropolis — with the exception of our highly-favoured and long-tried brother, James Wells, of the Surrey Tabernacle — who had such crowded auditories, and continued overflowing congregations, as Mr Spurgeon has. But then, very solemn questions arise: What is he doing? Whose servant is he? What proof does he give that, instrumentally, his is a heart-searching, a Christ-exalting, a truth-unfolding, a sinner-converting, a church-feeding, a soul-saving ministry?'

This was mild compared with the following month's edition of the same publication. A long letter bearing the signature 'Job' (Spurgeon believed the writer was the James Wells referred to above) contained the following statements:

'And yet further than all this, Mr Spurgeon was, so says the
Vessel, brought to know the Lord when he was only fifteen
years old. Heaven grant it may prove to be so — for the young
man's sake, and for that of others also! But I have — most
solemnly have — my doubts as to the divine reality of his
conversion. I do not say — it is not for me to say — that he is
not a regenerated man, but this I do know, that there are
conversions which are not of God.' After making that most
serious charge as to Spurgeon's conversion, the writer
dismissed his ministry by asserting that it was 'most awfully
deceptive', and that he 'is simply deceiving others with the
deception wherewith he deceives himself'.

Many other letters, for and against, followed. The *Ipswich
Express* of February 1855 included a letter with a particular
accusation: 'Actually, I hear, the other Sunday, the gifted
divine had the impudence, before preaching, to say, as there
were many young ladies present, that he was engaged — that
his heart it was another's, he wished them clearly to understand that — that he might have no presents sent him, no
attentions paid him, no worsted slippers worked for him by the
young ladies present. I suppose the dear divine has been
rendered uncomfortable by the fondness of his female audi-
tors; at any rate, such is the impression he wishes to leave.'

Such attacks upon a very young and inexperienced minister
were amazing. He felt deeply these slanders but he had the
wisdom to see beyond the petty jealousies of men. He knew
that 'We wrestle not against flesh and blood', and so was able
rightly to assess the situation. 'The devil is roused, the church
is awakening, and I am now counted worthy to suffer for
Christ's sake.' Spurgeon was one of a long line of gospel
preachers who had suffered in the same way. He was neither
the first nor the last to have to face the slanders and lies of
outraged religious men. Perhaps we can best understand these
attacks by referring to a letter in the *Essex Standard* of April
1855 from a supporter of Spurgeon. He wrote, 'The pulpit is
now too much abused by the mere display of intellect; instead
of the indignant burst of a Luther against the iniquities of

mankind, we have only the passive disapprobation of the silvery-tongued man of letters. The preachers address their cold, "packed-in-ice" discourses to the educated portion of their audience; and the majority, the uneducated poor, are unable, in these "scientific" sermons, to learn the way of holiness, from the simple fact that they are above their comprehension.

'Mr Spurgeon goes to the root of the evil; his discourses are such as a child can understand, and yet filled with the most elevating philosophy and sound religious instruction. Taking the Word as his only guide, and casting aside the writings — however antiquated — of fallible men, he appeals to the heart, not to the head; puts the living truth forcibly before the mind, gains the attention, and then, as he himself says, fastens in the bow the messenger shaft, which, by the blessing and direction of the Almighty, strikes home to the heart of the sinner.'

It is often said that there is no such thing as bad publicity. This certainly proved to be true at New Park Street. The stories of Spurgeon in the press brought many curious listeners to the church. This became so marked that Spurgeon noted that 'Great numbers of the converts of those early days came as a direct result of the slanders with which I was so mercilessly assailed.'

11.
The work goes on

God's hand was obviously upon this young man, and so in spite of the opposition the work at New Park Street prospered. The building was far too small and for two periods in 1855 and 1856 the church had to use the Exeter Hall in the Strand, and then for three years (1856-1859) they made their home in the Music Hall in the Royal Surrey Gardens. A third period was spent in the Exeter Hall from December 1859 to March 1861. During this time a new chapel was being built and the Metropolitan Tabernacle was opened in 1861.

The Minute Book from the church meeting on 6 May contains the following acknowledgement: 'We, the undersigned members of the church lately worshipping in New Park Street Chapel, but now assembling in the Metropolitan Tabernacle, Newington, desire with overflowing hearts to make known and record the loving-kindness of our faithful God. We asked in faith, but our Lord has exceeded our desires, for not only was the whole sum given us, but far sooner than we had looked for it. Truly, the Lord is good, and worthy to be praised. We are ashamed of ourselves that we ever doubted him; and we pray that, as a church and as individuals, we may be enabled to trust in the Lord at all times with confidence, so that in quietness we may possess our souls. In the name of our God we set up our banner. Oh that Jehovah-Jireh may also be unto us Jehovah-Shammah and Jehovah-Shalom! To Father, Son

The Metropolitan Tabernacle

and Holy Ghost we offer praise and thanksgiving, and we set to our seal that God is true.'

Spurgeon ministered at the Tabernacle until his death on 31 January 1892. It was a remarkable ministry which saw the conversion of countless numbers of sinners. This was always the great burden of Spurgeon's heart. He was pre-eminently a preacher, with the preacher's concern for lost souls. His ministry was far wider than the London church, and he preached all over the country. Every week one of his sermons was printed and these went all over the world. By 1899 over a hundred million copies of Spurgeon's sermons had been distributed in twenty-three languages. And this is not merely something that happened in the past, because these sermons are still being printed today.

Preaching, then, was the centre of Spurgeon's ministry, but his work was broader. He founded the Pastors' College for the training of men for the ministry. The value of this college can be appreciated from the following words of one of the students: 'In those days, the president was in his prime. His step was firm, his eyes were bright, his hair was dark and abundant, his voice full of sweetest music and sacred merriment. Before him were gathered a hundred men from all parts of the United Kingdom, and not a few from beyond the seas. They were brought together by the magic of his name, and the attraction of his personal influence. His fame had gone out into all lands. His sermons were published in almost all languages. Many sitting before him were his own sons in the faith. Among the students he was at ease, as a father in the midst of his own family. The brethren loved him, and he loved them.'

Yet another important ministry was the establishing of the Stockwell Orphanage. Such a work of necessity involved a great deal of money and Spurgeon approached this, as he did everything in his life, with an unwavering faith in the goodness of God. He said in 1867, 'I hope the day may soon come when the noble example which has been set by our esteemed brother, Mr Muller, of Bristol, will be more constantly followed in all the Lord's work; for, rest assured that, if we will but "believe

to see", we shall see great things. I cannot forbear mentioning
to you tonight what God has enabled us to see of late as a
church. We met together one Monday night, as you will
remember, for prayer concerning the Orphanage; and it was
not a little remarkable that on the Saturday of that week the
Lord should have moved some friend, who knew nothing of
our prayers, to give five hundred pounds to that object. It
astonished some of you that, on the following Monday night,
God should have influenced another to give six hundred
pounds! When I told you of that, at the next prayer meeting,
you did not think perhaps that the Lord had something else in
store, and that, the following Tuesday, another friend would
come with five hundred pounds! It was just the same in the
building of this tabernacle. We were a few poor people when
we commenced, but still we moved on by faith, and never went
into debt. We trusted in God, and the house was built, to the
eternal honour of him who hears and answers prayers. And,
mark you, it will be so in the erection of this Orphan Home. We
shall see greater things than these if only our faith will precede
our sight. But if we go upon the old custom of our general
societies, and first look out for a regular income, and get our
subscribers, and send round our collectors, and pay our per-
centages — that is, do not trust God, but trust our subscribers
— if we go by rule, we shall see very little, and have no room
for believing. But if we shall just trust God, and believe that he
never did leave a work that he put upon us, and never sets us
to see a thing without meaning to help us through with it, we
shall soon see that the God of Israel still lives, and that his arm
is not shortened.'

Controversy

The preaching, college and orphanage were a great source of
satisfaction and joy to Spurgeon, but he also knew great trials
and suffering. The last seven years of his life were marked by
very poor health. In fact long before those last few years the

The Stockwell Orphanage

strain and pressure of the work had been taking its toll upon him. He wrote in 1871, 'The highest medical authorities are agreed that only long rest can restore me. I wish it were otherwise.' Then in 1879 he said, 'During the time that I have been preaching the gospel in this place, I have suffered many times from severe sickness and frightful mental depression, sinking almost to despair. Almost every year I have been laid aside for a season; for flesh and blood cannot bear the strain, at least such flesh and blood as me. I believe the affliction was necessary to me and has answered salutary ends; but I would, if it were God's will, escape from frequent illness: that must be according to his will and not mine.'

This physical suffering was very painful but it was not to be compared with the mental and spiritual anguish he suffered during what is known as the 'Down-grade Controversy'. This was so painful that his wife believed his fight for the faith had cost him his life.

For some time Spurgeon had been greatly disturbed at the way the nonconformist churches were tolerating liberal theology and the attendant rejection of the authority of Scripture. In 1887 he wrote a series of articles on this in his magazine, *The Sword and the Trowel*, in which he said, 'Attendance at places of worship is declining, and reverence for holy things is vanishing; and we solemnly believe this to be largely attributable to the scepticism which has flashed from the pulpit and spread among the people.'

He went on to face the real issue: 'It now becomes a serious question how far those who abide by the faith once delivered to the saints should fraternize with those who have turned aside to another gospel. Christian love has its claims, and divisions are to be shunned as grievous evils; but how far are we justified in being in confederacy with those who are departing from the truth?'

This was a most serious charge, but it was ignored by the Baptists, and Spurgeon resigned from the Baptist Union on 28 October 1887. He faced bitter criticism not only from those who had always opposed him, but even from former friends.

The fight for the truth cost Spurgeon greatly. Others knew he was right but kept silent. But it was not in the nature of the man to be silent when the gospel was 'being buried beneath the boiling mud-showers of modern heresy'. He said, 'I am quite willing to be eaten by dogs for the next fifty years but the more distant future shall vindicate me!'

Postscript

Charles Haddon Spurgeon died in Mentone, in the south of France, on 31 January 1892, and thus ended one of the most remarkable ministries England has known. Countless thousands were brought to Christ through his preaching and during his pastorate in London 14,691 were received into membership.

Throughout his ministry Spurgeon's prime concern was for the glory of his Saviour in the salvation of souls. It is appropriate therefore that we close with some of his words to the unsaved. 'Reader, are you unsaved? Have you experienced any noteworthy deliverances? Then adore and admire the free grace of God, and pray that it may lead you to repentance! Are you enquiring for the way of life? Remember the words *Dei Gratia* (by the grace of God), and never forget that by grace we are saved. Grace always presupposes unworthiness in its object. The province of grace ceases where merit begins; what a cheering word is this to those of you who have no worth, no merit, no goodness whatever! Crimes are forgiven, and follies are cured by our Redeemer out of mere free favour. The word grace has the same meaning as our common term 'gratis': Wickliffe's prayer was, 'Lord save me gratis.' No works can purchase or procure salvation, but the heavenly Father giveth freely, and upbraideth not.

'Grace comes to us from faith in Jesus. Whoever believes on him is not condemned. O sinner, may God give you grace to look to Jesus and live. Look now, for today is the accepted time!'